Sexual Abuse
and Residential Treatment

Sexual Abuse and Residential Treatment

Wander de C. Braga, MD
Raymond Schimmer, MAT
Editors

Routledge
Taylor & Francis Group

LONDON AND NEW YORK

Sexual Abuse and Residential Treatment has also been published as *Residential Treatment for Children & Youth,* Volume 11, Number 1 1993.

First published 1993 by The Harworth Press, Inc.

2 Park Square, Milton Park, Abingdon, Oxon OX14 4RN
711 Third Avenue, New York, NY 10017, USA

Routledge is an imprint of the Taylor & Francis Group, an informa business

First issued in paperback 2016

Library of Congress Cataloging-in-Publication Data

Sexual abuse and residential treatment / Wander de C. Braga, Raymond Schimmer, editors.
    p. cm.
    Includes bibliographical references and index.
    ISBN 978-1-560-24475-2 (hbk)
    1. Child psychotherapy–Residential treatment. 2. Adolescent psychotherapy–Residential treatment. 3. Child molesting–Prevention. 4. Children–Sexual behavior. 5. Teenagers–Sexual behavior. I. Braga, Wander de C. II. Schimmer, Raymond.
RJ504.5.S49 1993
618.92'85836–dc20
                                              93-2422
                                                CIP

ISBN 978-1-138-98171-3 (pbk)

INDEXING & ABSTRACTING

Contributions to this publication are selectively indexed or abstracted in print, electronic, online, or CD-ROM version(s) of the reference tools and information services listed below. This list is current as of the copyright date of this publication. See the end of this section for additional notes.

- *Applied Social Sciences Index & Abstracts, (ASSIA)*, Bowker-Saur Limited, 60 Grosvenor Street, London W1X 9DA, England

- *Cambridge Scientific Abstracts, Health & Safety Science Abstracts*, Cambridge Information Group, 7200 Wisconsin Avenue #601, Bethesda, MD 20814

- *Child Development Abstracts & Bibliography*, University of Kansas, 2 Bailey Hall, Lawrence, KS 66045

- *Criminal Justice Abstracts*, Willow Tree Press, 15 Washington Street, 4th Floor, Newark, NJ 07102

- *Criminology, Penology and Police Science Abstracts*, Kugler Publications, P.O. Box 11188, 1001 GD Amsterdam, The Netherlands

- *Exceptional Child Education Resources (ECER), (online through DIALOG and hard copy)*, The Council for Exceptional Children, 1920 Association Drive, Reston, VA 22091

- *Index to Periodical Articles Related to Law*, University of Texas, 727 East 26th Street, Austin, TX 78705

(continued)

- *International Bulletin of Bibliography on Education*, Proyecto B.I.B.E./Apartado 52, San Lorenzo del Escorial, Madrid, Spain

- *Inventory of Marriage and Family Literature (online and hard copy)*, National Council on Family Relations, 3989 Central Avenue NE, Suite 550, Minneapolis, MN 55421

- *Mental Health Abstracts (online through DIALOG)*, IFI/Plenum Data Company, 3202 Kirkwood Highway, Wilmington, DE 19808

- *Psychological Abstracts (PsycINFO)*, American Psychological Association, P.O. Box 91600, Washington, DC 20090-1600

- *Sage Family Studies Abstracts*, Sage Publications, Inc., 2455 Teller Road, Newbury Park, CA 91320

- *Social Planning/Policy & Development Abstracts (SOPODA)*, Sociological Abstracts, Inc., P.O. Box 22206, San Diego, CA 92192-0206

- *Social Work Research & Abstracts*, National Association of Social Workers, 750 First Street NW, 8th Floor, Washington, DC 20002

- *Sociological Abstracts (SA)*, Sociological Abstracts, Inc., P.O. Box 22206, San Diego, CA 92192-0206

- *Sociology of Education Abstracts*, Carfax Publishing Company, P.O. Box 25, Abingdon, Oxfordshire OX14 3UE, United Kingdom

- *Special Educational Needs Abstracts*, Carfax Information Systems, P.O. Box 25, Abingdon, Oxfordshire OX14 3UE, United Kingdom

(continued)

SPECIAL BIBLIOGRAPHIC NOTES

related to indexing, abstracting, and library access services

☐ indexing/abstracting services in this list will also cover material in the "separate" that is co-published simultaneously with Haworth's special thematic journal issue or DocuSerial. Indexing/abstracting usually covers material at the article/chapter level.

☐ monographic co-editions are intended for either non-subscribers or libraries which intend to purchase a second copy for their circulating collections.

☐ monographic co-editions are reported to all jobbers/wholesalers/approval plans. The source journal is listed as the "series" to assist the prevention of duplicate purchasing in the same manner utilized for books-in-series.

☐ to facilitate user/access services all indexing/abstracting services are encouraged to utilize the co-indexing entry note indicated at the bottom of the first page of each article/chapter/contribution.

☐ this is intended to assist a library user of any reference tool (whether print, electronic, online, or CD-ROM) to locate the monographic version if the library has purchased this version but not a subscription to the source journal.

☐ individual articles/chapters in any Haworth publication are also available through the Haworth Document Delivery Services (HDDS).

Sexual Abuse and Residential Treatment

CONTENTS

ABOUT THE EDITORS

Wander de C. Braga, MD, is Director of Psychiatric and Medical Services at Parsons Child and Family Center in Albany, New York. He also serves as Assistant Director of Training in the Child Psychiatry Division of the Albany Medical College Department of Psychiatry. In the past twenty years he has focused his clinical activities on the long-term treatment of severely disturbed residentially placed children and adolescents. His interest for the area of child sexual abuse relates to the over-representation of this special population in residential treatment centers. Dr. Braga teaches various disciplines including medicine, psychology, psychiatry, social work, and child care.

Raymond Schimmer, MAT, is Assistant Executive Director for Residence and Education at Parsons Child and Family Center in Albany, New York. In this position, he is responsible for overseeing all internal investigations of abuse allegations. Over the past several years, Mr. Schimmer has developed policies and procedures to guide and train educational, clinical, and child care staff. He previously worked at Tufts-New England Medical Center's psychiatric day hospital for children in Boston and at the Walker School in Needham, Massachusetts.

ABOUT THE CONTRIBUTORS

Eliana Gil, PhD, is a well-known lecturer, author and clinician who received her doctorate from the California Graduate School of Family Psychology in San Rafael, CA. Early in her career she became interested in the problem of child abuse, an interest she maintains to this day. She was President of the California Professional Society on the Abuse of Children in the years 1987-1989, and she continues on the Board of Directors of this organization. She was formerly Director of Gil and Associates, a child abuse treatment program, and Director of the Contra Costa Child Abuse Prevention Council. She has been on the advisory board of the National Resource Center on Child Sexual Abuse and she is the founder and senior advisor of A Step Forward, a child abuse treatment and training program, where she maintains her private practice.

Toni Cavanagh Johnson, PhD, is a licensed clinical psychologist in private practice in South Pasadena, CA. Dr. Johnson has written extensively on childhood sexuality and problems of sexual abuse of children. She provides consultation and training on these matters to protective services, police, probation departments, mental health practitioners, foster and adoptive parents, as well as residential facilities.

Wayne T. Aoki, PhD, is currently Director of Research at The Sycamores, a residential treatment program in Altadena, CA. Formerly, Dr. Aoki was Director of Clinical Services at the same agency, where he was responsible for overseeing the development of behavioral treatment plans for the young boys receiving services in that agency.

Jonathan E. Ross, MA, is Director of the Waypoint Program at New Hope, Inc. in Summerville, SC and speaks internationally on the subject of adolescent sex offenders. The Waypoint Program was recently featured in the simulcast television documentary "Scared Silent" narrated by Oprah Winfrey. Mr. Ross has developed several other specialized sex offender programs in both correctional, outpatient and residential settings. He has been providing assessment and treatment services to adult and adolescent sexual offenders since 1979 and was appointed to the National Task Force on Juvenile Sexual Offending in 1985. He received both his Bachelor and Master of Arts degrees in psychology from Connecticut College where he graduated an elected member of Phi Beta Kappa.

Mark P. de Villier, MSW, LPC, is Executive Director of New Hope, Inc. which, in addition to the Waypoint Program, houses a general psychiatric unit. He has been Director of Clinical Services as well as Director of Residential Services there since 1984. Mr. de Villier has worked with emotionally disturbed adolescents and their families as well as in substance abuse counseling for fourteen years. He received his Bachelor of Science degree in psychology from the College of Charleston and his Master of Social Work degree from the University of South Carolina.

Beth Caldwell, MS, and Erlinda Rejino, MS, work for the New York State Office of Mental Health, Bureau of Children and Families. Their responsibilities include overseeing 15 state-operated inpatient programs (567 beds); 17 residential treatment facilities (460 beds); and 15 community and crisis residence programs (110 beds).

Ms. Caldwell received her MS in Psychology and Administration from the University of Nebraska. Ms. Rejino is in the process of completing her MS in Community Psychology. They both work to ensure that all children can be raised in stable families or family-like environments; they have also devoted large amounts of time in recent years to ensure safe and therapeutic environments for children who, for relatively short periods of time, must be hospitalized or who reside in congregate care settings.

David A. Nevin, PhD, has had over twenty years of experience in residential treatment as Staff Psychologist and Consultant at Parsons Child and Family Center, Albany, NY. Currently, he also works with the Sex Abuse Prevention Program and the Juvenile Sex Offender Program, both at the St. Anne's Institute, in the same city. Besides his private practice of clinical psychology, he has been a speaker in many professional presentations as well as a consultant to many other therapeutic settings.

Foreword

This volume reflects the impact of context on point of view. The articles included address the topic of sexual abuse in residential settings from the contextual perspectives of development; values; the therapeutic milieu; safety; training; and clinical experience. We intentionally sought authors who would produce disparate and occasionally conflicting ideas as they addressed the general topic through a specific subject. We wished to convey some of the ferment evident today in philosophy and practice as related to this area. We wished as well to avoid implying the existence of a reliable orthodoxy. The theme of sex invariably evokes powerful emotional responses as well as ethical dilemmas–all of which connotes a disparity of perspective that is inevitable and necessary at this time.

We hope that the reader will find these articles helpful, particularly from the practice view-point. By developing a firmer grasp of the framework in which the complex matter of sexual abuse is embedded, practitioners will be better equipped to introduce concrete changes in their programs, thereby enhancing quality of services.

Wander de C. Braga, MD
Raymond Schimmer, MAT
Editors

[Haworth co-indexing entry note]: "Foreword." Braga, Wander de C., and Raymond Schimmer. Co-published simultaneously in *Residential Treatment for Children & Youth*, (The Haworth Press, Inc.) Vol. 11, No. 1, 1993, p. *xix*; and: *Sexual Abuse and Residential Treatment* (ed: Wander de C. Braga, and Raymond Schimmer) The Haworth Press, Inc., 1993, p. *xv*. Multiple copies of this article/ chapter may be purchased from The Haworth Document Delivery Center. Call 1-800-3-HAWORTH (1-800-342-9678) between 9:00 - 5:00 (EST) and ask for DOCUMENT DELIVERY CENTER.

xv

Preface

In 1978 the National Center on Child Abuse and Neglect awarded a grant to the San Francisco Child Abuse Council (in cooperation with the Department of Social Services) to study the incidence and circumstances of "institutional abuse." I served as Assistant Director with the two-year pilot project and provided training to hundreds of foster parents, group home and residential treatment center staff in California, Arizona, Hawaii and Guam.

When the grant was announced, we approached a number of administrators within institutions and asked for their cooperation. We encountered alarmed and defensive responses. Administrators were acutely suspicious about the expressed goals of our project: Were we going to uncover problems in the institutions and make them public? If problems were made public, most administrators feared the bad publicity would gravely interfere with their referral base. How could outsiders understand the complexity and challenge of providing out-of-home care services?

We were initially surprised by this defensive posture and yet we came to understand that many institutions were quite protective and skeptical of outside interference. Breaking the resistance to cooperate was our first task. Our intent was to gain access to line-workers, administrators and managers who would confide any difficulties they experienced with child abuse within their facilities. Eventually, personnel described their experiences in an honest and straightfor-

[Haworth co-indexing entry note]: "Preface." Gil, Eliana. Co-published simultaneously in *Residential Treatment for Children & Youth*, (The Haworth Press, Inc.) Vol. 11, No. 1, 1993, pp. *xxi-xxiv*; and: *Sexual Abuse and Residential Treatment* (ed: Wander de C. Braga, and Raymond Schimmer) The Haworth Press, Inc., 1993, pp. *xvii-xxii*. Multiple copies of this article/chapter may be purchased from The Haworth Document Delivery Center. Call 1-800-3-HA-WORTH (1-800-342-9678) between 9:00 - 5:00 (EST) and ask for DOCUMENT DELIVERY CENTER.

xvii

ward manner. They articulated difficulties with staff training and supervision; vague and unclear policies (for example, about the use of time-out and restraint): and a closed climate where problems could not be discussed. In particular, young untrained staff found that they often felt compelled to keep their concerns or countertransference responses to themselves for fear others might chastise them or else place their jobs at risk. As a result of these conversations with personnel at 24-hour institutions, we clarified the definition of institutional abuse to include not only individual staff-child abuse of any type, but also program or system responses that created the potential for abusive practices and policies (Gil, 1982). An example of a program abuse might be an inadequate nutritional program; a system abuse might be multiple placements for children and an undefined and unregulated placement plan.

An additional focus of our study was to assess the incidence of out-of-home care abuse and neglect. We realized quickly that this was an impossible task because specific incidents of child abuse were usually ignored, or dealt with internally; another common practice was to make reports to placement or licensing agencies not authorized to receive suspected reports of child abuse and neglect. Placement and licensing personnel frequently responded in inconsistent and idiosyncratic ways. For example, a licensing official told us that he would not respond to a report from an institution unless there were "blood and guts on the wall." When talking with placement personnel they said they frequently handled reports of abuse by removing children from the facility and placing the facility name in an "alert" file. These files were not routinely circulated among staff so if one staff member was cognizant of a problem, there was no guarantee that any other placement workers would be privy to this information. Needless to say, we identified many problems that contributed to inconsistency, in both data-keeping and interventions in allegations of abuse within institutions. We also stimulated critical and useful discussion among the Region IX out-of-home care facilities.

What has happened since that time is quite remarkable! Great efforts have been made "from the inside" to articulate and address concerns and problems. The 1990 annual conference of the American Association of Children's Residential Centers highlighted the topic of sexual abuse in residential centers and proposed a number of suggested program policies and procedures to prevent its occurrence. Leadership from within residential centers has been established which actively heightens awareness and provides forums for the development of responsible and proactive policies and programs.

In this volume, we enjoy honest and stimulating discussion of issues related to safety and prevention of abuse in residential care. The book offers a comprehensive and state-of-the art compilation of articles on the incidence, training and program policies, specialized concerns, and suggested procedures for child abuse prevention, assessment, and intervention within residential care. Unique in this volume is the straightforward and practical advice that generates only from individuals who know the problems first-hand and have the expertise to demonstrate functional guidance and leadership.

The book begins with a chapter by Johnson and Aoki on the sexual behaviors of latency-age children in residential treatment. Johnson has been instrumental in providing early information on children who molest in the general population (Johnson, 1988, 1989) and now combines with Aoki to study the sexual behaviors of children in residential care using a sexual behavior checklist she developed. The study shows that residential staff will encounter natural and expectable sexual behaviors in their residents, as well as more problematic sexual behaviors, not uncommon for children with histories of physical and sexual abuse. In particular they found that children with both physical and sexual abuse in their backgrounds are very high risk for sexual acting-out behaviors. Because of these findings, Johnson and Aoki urge staff to develop comprehensive training regarding childhood sexuality; training must address staff countertransference problems. They urge that institutions define a philosophy on childhood sexuality which defines the boundaries of physical contact between staff and residents, and residents among themselves. In addition, when children exhibit problematic sexual behaviors, specific and detailed responses must be anticipated and defined. Many specific suggestions regarding case management, behavioral interventions, and treatment planning are offered in this compelling and informative opening chapter.

Raymond Schimmer follows with a fascinating and thought-provoking discussion about how best to govern the sexual behaviors of children in residential treatment centers. As he aptly states, agencies can err by attempting to eliminate any and all sexual activity and develop a suppressive and rigid climate. On the other hand, failing to develop some policies on sexual behaviors among residents can lead to problematic, even dangerous, situations. Schimmer exposes both sides of many issues. In so doing, he clearly demonstrates the complexity of developing effective policies and responses. Policies must respect children's rights to important behavioral expression and development, while teaching and fostering respect for the rights of others.

Caldwell and Rejino set the premise that many child residents are placed in out-of-home care due to their histories of abuse and neglect and may struggle with victim/victimizer dynamics; agencies must therefore ensure safe environments for residents. They propose a range of clear and specific administrative and clinical practices that enhance and ensure safety. They list five factors identified by the New York Office of Mental Health as critical to keeping children safe from harmful sexual activity in residential care. These five factors are administrative understanding and commitment; environmental factors; staff attitudes; clinical factors and the investigatory and incident review processes. They conclude that a residential environment that is safe from sexual exploitation and abuse correlates with the ability of the administrative and clinical staff to "review, re-think, and introduce changes in various critical areas."

Nevin asserts that residential centers have been largely reactive to critical incidents and outside regulators in response to concerns about sexual abuse, and challenges residential staff to take a leadership role in both articulating and addressing problems. The focus of his article is one of the staples of effective prevention efforts: training. Nevin suggests that training must be categorized and designed to meet the specific needs of myriad caretakers involved in residential care. Nevin notes that staff supervision, professionalism in child care, organizational issues and staff recruitment are among the most important variables in preventing institutional abuse.

Ross and de Villier discuss development and implementation of an adolescent offender program in residential treatment centers. Intake procedures, selection of staff, living units for sex offenders, and guidelines for resident and staff safety are presented as critical considerations in developing such programs. Strong emphasis is placed on safety concerns to enhance and support treatment plans. Recommendations are congruent with findings of the National Task Force on Juvenile Sexual Offending.

The final two chapters by Braga focus on allegations of sexual abuse in residential programs, and reveal the intricacy of these recently-documented situations. Braga uses vivid clinical examples to illustrate how allegations of abuse in residential centers occur within the context of complex personal, clinical, staff-related and familial variables which must be disentangled to assess accurately. The second of these chapters discusses definitional concerns, mandated reporting, investigatory practices and allocation of resources. Braga calls for a cooperative rather than adversarial relationship between residential programs and external monitoring bodies.

Residential center boards of directors, administrators, managers, clinical and caretaking personnel face unique challenges in their efforts to provide safe, practical, and therapeutic responses to children in their care. Children who enter residential centers have experienced a range of stressful and overwhelming situations including family violence, child abuse, drug use, economic duress, parental physical or mental illness, and so on. Consequently, children may have a variety of symptomatic and acting-out behaviors that require specific interventions. Children with histories of abuse or exposure to violence may indentify with the aggressor and internalize conflicts regarding victim/victimizer dynamics. These difficulties and others require clear and specific treatment with an underlying philosophy of keeping children safe from harm to self or others. In recent years, attempts have been made from within residential centers to prepare for potential abuse incidents between residents or between staff and residents. A more open and less guarded atmosphere has evolved in which institutions recognize the benefit of anticipating abuse possibilities and preparing a response rather than reacting to incidents after the fact. In addition to suicidal or violent behaviors in residents, staff have expressed concern over the occurrence of problematic sexual behaviors in their residents. As this book explains, sexuality cannot be placed on the back burner while children are in residential care; therefore, normal and expectable sexual experimentation may surface, as well as problematic and potentially harmful sexual behaviors commonly associated with traumatized children. The dilemma for residential centers is how to support natural and expectable sexual development without overlooking problematic sexual behaviors that can result in an unsafe environment of sexual exploitation or abuse.

This book is replete with precise and practical suggestions for creating a safe and healthy environment. Emphasis is placed on the training of staff on issues of childhood sexuality, child abuse, and appropriate interventions.

The potential for child abuse to occur in residential centers is undisputed. What this book reflects is a growing interest in prevention and intervention, originating from within the residential treatment community itself. Its approach to this problem is frank, candid, and acutely sensitive to the actual realities and circumstances that can contribute to the emergence of abusive situations.

The climate of defensiveness and denial has been broken. This book is an important contribution to the literature on abuse within institutions because it is based on thoughtful introspection by experienced authors who offer lucid and practical recommendations. It will be useful reading for anyone involved in the provision of out-of-home care services to children and their families.

Eliana Gil, PhD

REFERENCES

Gil, E. (1982). Institutional abuse of children in out-of-home home care. Child and Youth Care Review, 4, 7-13.

Johnson, T. C. (1988). Children who molest other children: Preliminary findings. Child Abuse and Neglect, 12, 219-229.

Johnson, T. C. (1989). Female child perpetrators: children who molest other children. Child Abuse and Neglect, 13, (4): 571-585.

Sexual Behaviors
of Latency Age Children
in Residential Treatment

Toni Cavanagh Johnson, PhD
Wayne T. Aoki, PhD

SUMMARY. One hundred and fifty eight children between the ages of 6 and 11 in residential treatment were assessed using measures designed to study their everyday problem behaviors as well as their sexual behaviors. The frequency of natural and expectable sexual behaviors is given, as well as a description of more problematic sexual behaviors. The relationship between everyday problem behaviors and the childrens' rating on a scale to measure sexual functioning is described. Suggestions for training and supervision of child care workers and all residential staff regarding children's sexual problems are included.

Correspondence may be sent to Dr. Johnson at 1101 Fremont Avenue, Suite 104, South Pasadena, CA 91030. The authors gratefully acknowledge the wisdom of Anthony Blount, Kichea Burt, Wanda Green, Stephanie Hager, Deon Sutton and DeLynn Turner who are excellent caregivers for abused and neglected children. They also thank Miriam Birnham, Fern Grunberger and Linda Waters, who gave valuable input concerning the supervision of children and staff in residential facilities.

[Haworth co-indexing entry note]: "Sexual Behaviors of Latency Age Children in Residential Treatment." Johnson, Toni Cavanagh, and Wayne T. Aoki. Co-published simultaneously in *Residential Treatment for Children & Youth*, (The Haworth Press, Inc.) Vol. 11, No. 1, 1993, pp. 1-22; and: *Sexual Abuse and Residential Treatment* (ed: Wander de C. Braga, and Raymond Schimmer) The Haworth, Inc., 1993, pp. 1-22. Multiple copies of this article/chapter may be purchased from The Haworth Document Delivery Center. Call 1-800-3-HA-WORTH (1-800-342-9678) between 9:00 - 5:00 (EST) and ask for DOCUMENT DELIVERY CENTER.

1

Research on childhood sexual behavior is very scant (Gil & Johnson, 1993) and the concept of childhood sexuality poorly understood to date. Even a basic understanding of what is meant by child sexuality is lacking. For some, to acknowledge that children engage in any sort of sexual behaviors is difficult. Freud (1962) was among the first to foster the idea that children are sexual from birth, yet believed that children's sexuality was latent during the early school years. Many studies have demonstrated that Freud's belief in the latency period was incorrect (Finkelhor, 1983; Haugaard & Tilly, 1988; Goldman & Goldman, 1988). In fact, children engage in a variety of sexual behaviors from normal to pathological from their earliest years (Johnson, 1991b).

There has been an increased interest in understanding the differences between the sexual behaviors of children who have been abused and those who have not been abused (Friedrich, Gramsch et al., 1992). Research indicates that mothers of sexually abused children observed sexual behaviors in their children more frequently than the mothers of non-abused children (Friedrich, Gramsch et al., 1991; Friedrich, Gramsch et al., 1992). As many children in residential care have been sexually abused, it is valuable to understand the frequency and type of such behaviors.

Johnson (1991b) noted that there is a range of severity of sexual behavior problems in children in care. Some children who had been overstimulated sexually engaged in a wide range of sexual behaviors, expressed both towards adults and other children. Some children engaged in extensive, yet mutual, sexual behaviors while others molested other children.

As no previous studies were found, we presently became interested in studying the frequency and types of sexual behaviors observed by staff in latency-aged children living in residential facilities. The everyday behavior problems of the children were also studied.

METHOD

Subjects

The sample consisted of children between the ages of 6 and 11 years, residents of treatment centers from seven different states.[1]

These centers were selected based on the authors' personal knowledge of them, which may represent a bias. All centers that were asked, agreed to participate but due to procedural errors, the subjects from only nine centers were utilized.

Procedures

Agency administrators were first invited to participate by direct telephone contact. After the authors received an informal agreement to participate, a cover letter and four questionnaires were mailed, along with an article by one of the authors giving an overview of child sexual behaviors (Johnson, 1991). This article also gave background information for understanding one of the assessment instruments. Instructions were that direct care staff should complete the questionnaires.

Agencies responded by indicating the number of children who fit the study criteria; that a caregiver was well enough acquainted with the child's background and current functioning level to answer the questionnaires; and that the child would be within the study's age range at the completion of the evaluation. All mailed questionnaires were returned in about three months time. All agencies employed their own means of assuring the anonymity of their children. Participating administrators were assured that the information gathered would not be published on an agency-by-agency basis, as this might inhibit their candor about the sexual acting-out exhibited by children in their respective centers.

Instruments

Four instruments were utilized. The first was a general information sheet soliciting demographic data including age, sex, ethnicity, religion, family income, and a checklist of abuse history.

The second instrument was a standardized behavioral checklist (i.e., the parent form of the Child Behavior Checklist [Achenbach, 1991]), which has two parts. The first part assesses social competency and academic performance. The second is a checklist of 113 behavioral items broken down into eight factors ranging from "withdrawn/isolative" to "aggressive/delinquent" behaviors. The instructions indicate that behaviors should be noted if they occurred within the past six months. When scored, three overall scale scores are derived: the Total T score; an Externalizing T score; and an Internalizing T score. High "externalizing" scores tend to correlate with acting-out, aggressive behaviors, while high "internalizing" scores correlate with anxious, depressive profiles.

The third instrument was the Child Sexual Behavior Checklist (CSBCL). This instrument was developed by Johnson (Gil & Johnson, 1993) as an assessment tool for children with problematic sexual behaviors. Normative data is currently being collected. It consists of three parts and lists behaviors related to sex and sexuality, including those that may indicate the presence of sexual difficulty (e.g., disturbed bathroom behaviors). Part 1 consists of 150 items checked for both occurrence and frequency. The present study analyzed only for occurrence. The time frame for this instrument is the previous three months. Nevertheless, behaviors which "used to" occur but were not evident in the previous three months can be recorded. The 150 items survey both normal and pathological behaviors divided into 22 categories, ranging from items such as "interest in how babies are made" to "tries to touch the 'private parts' of adults." Part 2 is comprised of questions related to the child's background for the purpose of providing a context for the behaviors in Part 1. Part 3 is completed only for children engaging in sexual behaviors with other children and is utilized for planning treatment interventions. The fourth and final instrument is the Group Membership Scale. This is a new instrument developed by Johnson (1991b) that attempts to place children's sexual behavior on a continuum from "normal" sex play to coercive, sexually aggressive behaviors with others. Four groups are delineated on the continuum: (1) sex play; (2) sexually-reactive behaviors; (3) extensive mutual sexual behaviors; and (4) child perpetrating behaviors. Behavioral markers and complete descriptions are provided for each category.

RESULTS

Data for 158 children between the ages of 6 and 11 were used in the study. Table 1 presents the demographic data describing this population.

Table 1
Demographic Information Regarding 158 Children Ages 6 - 11 in
Residential Treatment Centers

Description	n	%
Sex		
Boys	133	84
Girls	25	16
Age		
6 - 7 years	28	18
8 - 9 years	50	32
10 - 11 years	80	51
Racial Groups		
Caucasian	113	72
African American	33	21
Asian	2	1
Native American	10	6
Ethnic Hispanic	16	10
Family Income		
Welfare	107	68
15K - 25K	38	24
26K plus	9	6
Unknown	4	3
Religious Affiliation		
Catholic	33	21
Protestant	30	19
Other	14	9
None	28	18
Unknown	53	34

By comparison, a national survey of children in residential treatment settings indicate that approximately 70% are boys and 30% are girls. Caucasians make up 70%, African-Americans 28%, and 2% are Asian or Native American. Hispanics as an ethnic group, represent 10% in these national statistics (Sunshine et al., 1991). The children in the present study appear similar, although our sample of girls is small. In addition, the current sample has a significant bias towards higher numbers of welfare recipients and low income families. While comparison data was not found, this appears to be representative of residential settings.

For analysis, the study sample was organized into four groups based upon abuse history: (1) physically abused; (2) sexually abused; (3) both physically and sexually abused; and (4) not abused. A One-Way ANOVA and Scheffe's Test for Multiple Comparisons (Roscoe, 1975) were used for statistical purposes, with the CSBCL (Gil & Johnson, 1992) and the Child Behavior Checklist (Achenbach, 1991) functioning as dependent measures of the children's behavior. Table 2 tabulates those measures.

Analyzing the CSBCL component of Table 2, children who had been both physically and sexually abused manifested significantly more sexualized behaviors than either the physically abused group $(F(3,154) = 6.28, p < .01)$, or the non-abused group $(F(3,154) = 6.26, p < .01)$. The both physically and sexually abused group approached, but did not meet significance at the .05 level, in its difference from the sexually abused group $(F(3,154) = 2.62, p < .10)$.

Analyzing the tabulated T-scores from the Child Behavior Checklist (Achenbach, 1991), abuse history did not differentiate children on any of the three CBCL scales. Average scores for all groups are relatively high, which is to be expected for this population (the mean for the general population is 50 with a standard deviation of approximately 10 for all three scales). However, when the scale comprised of sex items of the Child Behavior Checklist was analyzed (not shown in Table 2), a significant difference was found between the both physically and sexually abused group $(M = 67.3; sd = 14.0)$ and the non-abused group $(M = 57.2; sd = 10.4)$, $(F(3,154) = 3.43, p < .05)$. No significant differences were found on this scale between the sexual abuse group, the physically abused and non-abused groups. Physical abuse, when added to sexual abuse, tended to increase the scores when compared to the trauma of sexual abuse alone, yet the differences did not reach statistical significance.

The CSBCL correlated .62 with the sex problems scale of the Child Behavior Checklist, .52 with the Total T, .42 with the Internalizing scale T scores, and .36 with the Externalizing scale T scores (see note on Table 2 for a brief explanation of these scales).

Child care workers often express concern with the lack of normative data regarding the behaviors of the children in residential treatment centers. Table 3 shows the occurrence of specific sexual behaviors amongst the children under study.

Even though many of the behaviors seem natural and expected,

Table 2
Summary of Scores from the Child Sexual Behavior Checklist and the Child Behavior Checklist

Abuse History	n	CSBCL		CBCL*					
				Tot		Int		Ext	
		mean	sd	mean	sd	mean	sd	mean	sd
Physical and Sexual Abuse	83	41.6	27.3	70.4	10.5	67.7	10.9	69.2	12.1
Physical Abuse	31	21.1	13.6	66.5	10.1	64.3	10.2	65.5	11.0
Sexual Abuse	15	24.0	20.1	68.5	7.7	62.7	9.1	70.0	9.4
Non-abuse	29	20.9	12.1	69.5	8.1	66.7	8.3	69.5	12.1
TOTAL	158	32.1	24.3	69.3	9.9	66.4	10.3	68.6	11.8

*The CBCL derives 3 sets of scores: Tot: Total of all behaviors; Int: Internalizing behaviors characteristic of clinical depression; and Ext: Externalizing behaviors characterized by delinquent and aggressive behaviors found in clinical conduct disorders.

child care staff have typically reported that among residentially placed children, many of these behaviors take on a sexualized tone. Table 4 further describes some of the more problematic sexual behaviors of the children surveyed.

The percentage of children engaging in sexual behaviors (see Table 4) is cause for concern. Children are placed in residential care to provide them safety from abuse, behavioral containment and healing.

Agencies are concerned about the child-to-child sexual behaviors occurring in their programs. One question on the CSBCL asks how children engage other children in sexual behavior. In our responses, 53 children either did not engage other children in sexual behavior, or the caregiver failed to answer the question, or else, to the best of their knowledge, they were unaware if such behavior occurred. For the remaining 105 cases, Table 5 indicates the means by which the children engaged other children in sexual behaviors, as reported by the caregivers. Staff indicated that 42% of the children who engaged other children in sexual behaviors have serious or very serious sexual problems.

We discarded the usage of the Group Membership Scale in this study because of the small sample of completed scales. This was probably due to unclarity of our instructions to respondents.

DISCUSSION

The data indicate that latency-aged children in residential care engage in a wide range of sexual behaviors. Many of these behaviors involve other children and adults.

Comparison of Sex Behaviors of Abused Children

Friedrich (1992) developed a checklist of 35 problematic sexual behaviors and upon applying it found significant differences between non-abused and sexually abused children (in an outpatient setting) on 27 of the items. The CSBCL with over 150 sexual items from normal to pathological, found in this study a significant difference between the set of children who had been both sexually and

Table 3
Ten Most Frequently Reported Sexual or Sexualized Behaviors

Description	n	%
1. Asks for hugs from adults.	155	98
2. Uses swear words in an angry way.	154	97
3. Interest in differences between boys and girls.	130	82
4. Talks about sex with friends.	128	81
5. Acts in sexy way.	108	68
6. Wiggles bottom at others.	106	67
7. Acts sexually forward with children.	101	64
8. Likes to be held close to the chest of adults.	101	64
9. Shows "private parts" to children.	97	61
10. Tries to peek at children when they are in the bathroom or bedroom.	96	61

Table 4
Frequencies of Child Sexual Behaviors With Other Children and Adults

Description	n	%
1. Rubs the clothes/hair of adults.	91	58
2. Tries to touch "private parts" of children.	78	49
3. Grabs children's "private parts" then runs away.	56	35
4. Tries to rub the breasts of adults.	54	34
5. Tries to rub legs/thighs of children.	50	32
6. Tries to rub legs/thighs of adults.	45	28
7. Tries to pull down boy's/girl's pants.	38	24
8. Tries to touch the "private parts" of adults.	37	23
9. Puts mouth on "private parts" of children.	36	23
10. Tries to put penis in "private parts" of children.(boys only)	34	26
11. Tries to put hands up girl's skirts.	30	19
12. Tries to put penis in mouth of others. (boys only)	27	20
13. Tries to put finger in the "private parts" of children.	26	16
14. Tries to put objects in the vagina/anus of others.	23	15
15. Tries to suck the neck of children to give "hickey".	21	13
16. Tries to suck the neck of adults to give "hickey".	16	10
17. Grabs at adult's "private parts" and then runs away.	16	10
18. Tries to put mouth on the "private parts" of adults.	14	9
19. Tries to pull down men's pants.	10	6
20. Sticks tongue in mouth of adult.	10	6

Table 5
Frequency of Means by Which Children Engaged Other Children into
Sexual Activity. N = 105

Description of Means	n	%
1. Asked	74	70
2. Teased	32	30
3. Tricked	22	21
4. Bribed	20	19
5. Threatened	8	8
6. Physically Forced	8	8
7. Other	22	21

physically abused, and those children who had been physically abused only, or who had not been abused at all. The differences were not significant between children both physically and sexually abused and those only sexually abused, although they approached significance. When the scale of sex items of the Child Behavior Checklist was analyzed, significant differences were found between those both physically and sexually abused and the non-abused group, but no significant differences were found between the sexually abused group, the physically abused and non-abused group. These data suggest that physical abuse may be a significant contributor to the development of sexual behavior problems in sexually abused children.

The vast majority of children, 83 out of 158 in this sample, had been both physically and sexually abused while only 15 children could be isolated who had sustained sexual abuse alone. Thirty-one children sustained physical abuse alone and 29 non-abused children were found. We had hoped to compare our data with similar data collected by Friedrich (1992). The latter studied non-abused children living at home and sexually abused children in outpatient treatment. This comparison was not feasible due to our small sample size of children who sustained sexual abuse alone. The extent of multiple forms of abuse among residential children is noteworthy. In the future, this comparison might bring to light differences in outpatient and residential children, both sexually abused and non-abused, as to their sexual behaviors.

The T scores on the Child Behavior Checklist and the high levels of sexual behaviors on the CSBCL speak to the severe consequences of multiple forms of abuse on children who then require residential care. The severity of problems of all children in residential treatment can be seen from the high levels of problems as reflected by both measures for these children, regardless of the type of abuse.

Accuracy of Reporting Sexual Behaviors

When scrutinizing the CSBCL data, questions arose as to the apparent inconsistency of responses. While a staff person would mark extensive sexual behaviors for a child and indicate that this child bribed or threatened other children into sexual behaviors, this staff would answer "not sure" to the question regarding whether the child had a sexual problem. While the institutions were asked to have on-line staff fill out the questionnaires, in some cases therapists replied instead. Although not statistically analyzed, it is clear that therapists did indicate more sexual behaviors and regarded them as more serious, as compared to the on-line staff. Attempting to verify this we conducted an informal survey of some supervisors and therapists who knew the children referenced and on whom line staff had filled out the earlier questionnaires. They confirmed that they were aware of more sexual behaviors and that the sexual problems were more severe on the children discussed. This discrepancy may be due to many factors, not the least of which is the amount of time devoted to filling out the form. Of concern though, from a training and supervision standpoint, is that some staff may normalize or deny the problems of some children. Staff may also be unprepared to label the child's behavior as a sexual problem. For some staff, acknowledging the sexual nature of many of these children's behaviors is very difficult. Staff interviewed suggested that extensive sexual acting out by children in their care might negatively impact the staff person's sense of competency. Embarrassment about observing the sexual behaviors, being touched themselves, or not having previously reported the behaviors, may have contributed to lower levels of reporting. It may also be that since therapists have greater access to the child's inner world and background, the incidence of sexual behavior problems is more easily accepted and therefore more often identified.

Future Research Using the CSBCL

Since the CSBCL lists many sexual behaviors which can be expected in all children, it is clear that in future research a weighing of responses to specific items on the CSBCL may increase its sensitivity to discriminate between different populations of children, if indeed differences do exist in residentially treated children.

Overall, the results of the study are only suggestive because of the non-random sample of institutions, the small sample size, and the tendency toward higher sexual behavior ratings by therapists than child care workers. More work is needed on the CSBCL, which has yet to develop validity and reliability standards.

Fulfilling the Need for Natural and Expectable Childhood Curiosity and Sexual Knowledge

A positive finding of this study is that expected behaviors related to sex and sexuality in young children (Johnson,1993) were found in the children in residential treatment. The natural curiosity of children regarding how babies are made (72% of sample), asking questions about sex (77% of sample), curiosity about the differences between boys and girls (82% of sample), "playing house" (61% of sample), "playing doctor" (37% of sample), and children who like to watch sexual activity on the television (65% of sample) were all evident in this population. Because empirical data on the frequency of these behaviors in home settings is unavailable, it is unclear whether these figures are consistent with those for non-residential children.

It is important that young children feel free to explore their own bodies and to discover the wide horizon of natural and healthy sexuality. This normal curiosity of young children must not be stymied. It is important for children to grow up with a healthy and balanced view of sex and sexuality so that puberty and adolescence may emerge as a time of measured exploration and experimentation. If sexual information and curiosity is forbidden or punished, it may be more highly sought. Sexual behaviors may then become imbued with a heightened salience, forcing thoughts, feelings and beliefs underground, only to explode to the surface with unfortunate repercussions. Caregivers are generally not trained in how to react to the normal sexual curiosity of children and, as the data from this study indicates, problematic behaviors are rather prevalent in residential children. Yet, in some instances, healthy touching, such as rubbing lotion on a child's feet or arms is discouraged for fear it will lead to sexual arousal. Sometimes, children are so closely watched that the challenge for the children is to evade the staffs' scrutiny. One 10-year old, in a group for children who molest, said, "they watch us like hawks, what are they so afraid of?"

While very difficult, agencies must attempt to allow natural and healthy sexual experimentation to evolve in young children in residential care. The introduction of curricula for sharing sexual information with latency-aged children is suggested. Within these curricula more than the physiology of sex should be discussed. Values, attitudes and feelings regarding sex and sexuality, natural and healthy sexual expression, and positive sexual relationships can also be explored, along with information on sexual stereotyping, boundaries (emotional, sexual and physical), sexual object choice, and sexual misuse and abuse.

Gathering Data on Sexual Behaviors

Very few residential facilities appear to gather data regarding the sexual behaviors of children using a checklist format, even in those cases where identifiable sexual behavior problems exist. The use of the CSBCL in this study demonstrated that important information can be culled from such a questionnaire, and that implicitly it is a powerful staff training tool. Many of the institutions involved in this study using the CSBCL checklist to gather data on sexual behaviors specifically indicated that using the CSBCL provided:

1. a focal point for discussing children's sexual behaviors, the staffs' feelings about same, and their feelings about working with children who engage in them;
2. a way of helping staff and the whole treatment team focus on the specific sexual behavior problems of an individual child, and all the children in the cottage or living unit;
3. a method of gauging the increase or decrease of sexual behavior problems of the child, if the measure is repeated over time;

4. a focal point for targeting specific sexual behaviors and developing specific behavior management plans in the residence and on the campus;
5. a way to measure the times of the day when a child has the most problems, if the measure is filled out by caregivers on different shifts;
6. an indication of a staff person's willingness or ability to accurately observe the sexual behaviors of the children in his or her care;
7. because the Child Sexual Behavior Checklist is divided into 22 sections, staff can see at a glance the major areas of concern for a child. In some children the sexualized behaviors are directed not at children, but at adults. This helps focus the treatment needs of the child and highlights the need to gather additional information from other staff members regarding the number of other adults toward whom the child is directing sexualized behaviors;
8. using the sexual behavior checklist helped some staff realize that they operated from the assumption that when they knew a child had been sexually abused, there would be an increase in sexual behavior problems. Staff were surprised that when documenting specific behaviors, many of the sexually abused children did not engage in a wider range of behaviors or with a higher frequency, than non-sexually abused children.

RECOMMENDATIONS

This study involved many hours of discussion with staff and supervisors from residential treatment facilities and yielded many valuable insights into their needs regarding work with children with sexual behavior problems. This, together with our experience and the results of the research, prompt the following recommendations.

Define the Philosophy and Working Assumptions of the Institution

Fundamental to the needs of the staff is the facility's definition of its philosophy of care and treatment, as well as the definition of policies addressing the work with children presenting problems in the area of sexuality. Before staff can effectively interact with children with sexual behavior problems they must be clear about the philosophy of the institution regarding the goals for these children. There must be a shared and defined set of assumptions about how to understand these childrens' behaviors and the needs that these children are expressing. The therapeutic modalities which will be utilized must be articulated throughout the community of workers so that all staff can assist in creating a therapeutic milieu. When there is a logical connection between the philosophy and practice, and when it is discussed in staff training, a basis for staff behavior and attitude is established. This will assist in creating a coherent atmosphere in the residence in which the children can feel comforted and contained and the staff can work in concert. Laying this foundation by training staff prior to their on-line employment will allow them to interact more effectively and comfortably with these children. Specific training is necessary for the on-line staff as well as counselors, social workers, psychologists, psychiatrists and all other people who come in direct or supervisory contact with children who have sexual behavior problems. In order to create an effective milieu for emotional and behavioral change, all staff regardless of their function, must share the same knowledge regarding the needs, goals and expectations for these children.

Define the Boundaries Regarding Touch

Fundamental to our understanding of the needs of children is the importance of physical contact with nurturing caregivers. There is no doubt that this is critical. Yet, campuses may need to examine their assumptions about physical contact between staff and children and how this is operationalized.

It is interesting to note that this research indicates that 155 of 158 children asked for hugs from staff on a regular basis. On many residential campuses children give and receive hugs from a vast multitude of adults. In some cases, children approach children with whom they have virtually no contact and ask for a hug. When asked, some children in these residential facilities respond that a hug from one person is the same as a hug from another. This may indicate an indiscriminate aspect to children's attachments. In the current sample, 58% of children were assessed as showing indiscriminate friendliness towards unfamiliar adults.

Some children have mistakenly learned that the most important aspect of getting or receiving a hug is that there is a request for the contact. The connection between having certain feelings which would make a hug feel good or consoling, and requesting the hug, is often missed. Children say they ask for a hug when they see someone, not necessarily when they feel sad or excited or are celebrating something.

Some staff do not like to hug children with whom they do not have a relationship, but feel compelled, if asked appropriately. Additionally, some staff feel they are denying the child a fundamental need, if they do not respond to all requests for hugs. Others acknowledge that giving hugs is basic to their confidence that they are helping the children and also adding to their enjoyment of their work. Some staff report feeling sexually violated by some children's physical contact. Confusion regarding hugging can lead to overindulgent, angry or punitive responses.

There is a great deal of complexity to the hugging of children on campus. This is further elucidated by a 10-year old boy who constantly asked for hugs from everyone he met. There seemed to be no pattern to his requests. He did not ask for hugs when he was happy, sad, mad or in distress. He just asked everyone, known or unknown, for hugs. As this became more apparent, it was decided that he would be asked to choose one staff person from whom he would receive and to whom he would give hugs. Everyone was surprised by his choice, including the caregiver who he selected, as she had no special relationship to him at all. After some time, it became known (he bragged to a fellow resident) that the reason for his selection was his height in relation to the height and size of her breasts.

Developing a policy regarding hugging must take into account the needs of the children and the staff. Suggestions have been made to limit hugs to cottage staff. Side-ways hugs have also been suggested to minimize against sexualization of this gesture.

Developing policies about touch and boundary regulation will also involve other behaviors which cause discomfort to staff such as: children putting their hands in the staff person's pockets; asking about their personal life; touching their breasts, buttocks and genitals; requests to hold hands; sitting on their laps; children exposing themselves (this can be very subtle); latency-aged girls surrounding a male staff; children masturbating, etc.

While physical contact and nurturing are essential, boundary issues are important for children to learn. As the children come from very distressed families with diffuse or, in some cases, nonexistent boundaries, the children need the adults to define the limits for physical touch. The use of the term "space invasion" or a "space invader" can lighten the tone regarding inappropriate touch and language in the residential setting. Some children appreciate the nuance of the extraterrestrial.

Many staff do not feel they can bring these physical boundary issues to team meetings for fear the childrens' sexual behaviors are their fault, or they will be blamed, or uncomfortably scrutinized by other staff. Asking for help to deal with such behaviors makes some staff feel inadequate: "I should know how to deal with this," or "maybe I brought it on." Some staff normalize the behavior and deny their own feelings. Confusion about the child's needs in regard to these boundary issues also precludes some staff from asking for help to stop the child. "I don't want to hurt the child."

Training for All Staff Members Who Interact with Children Presenting Problematic Sexual Behavior

The following suggestions are topics to supplement staff training already implemented in many institutions. The fundamental elements of training regarding child sexuality, child sexual behaviors and working with children with sexual behavior problems would include:

1. child sexuality. What it is and what is isn't;
2. natural and expectable sexual behaviors in children;
3. sexual behavior problems in children. The different types, etiology, problematic behaviors, characteristics of the children, associated problems, family dynamics, the meaning of sexual behaviors;

4. the assessment and management of sexual behavior problems in children;
5. treatment planning and case management for children with sexual behavior problems;
6. how to respond to the sexual behaviors of children (this should be *specific* and *detailed,* utilizing role plays);
7. values clarification for staff regarding the meanings to them of adult sexuality, child sexuality, masturbation, homosexuality, heterosexuality, bisexuality, contraception, abortion, sexual and physical abuse;
8. the parameters regarding physical contact between staff and children. The policy regarding staff hugging children and children hugging staff should be clear, as well as other forms of physical contact;
9. the causes of sexual abuse, the relationship between sexual, physical and emotional abuse, sexual abuse dynamics, the after effects of abuse;
10. transference and countertransference reactions between staff and children when the children have sexual and/or aggressive behavior problems. Staff should be helped to understand the possible effects on their emotional and sexual life of working with children with disturbed sexuality, and how their behaviors, thoughts and feelings can affect the children.

Treatment Team Meetings

Most residential facilities have treatment team meetings during which the on-line staff, therapists working with the children, social workers and, perhaps, a mental health consultant meet to discuss the treatment needs of the children. When working with children with sexual behavior problems, specific issues to address are:

1. Line staff create the milieu of the living units and are the most important resource for the children's recovery. They are with the children 24 hours a day. It is important for childrens' therapists, and consultants to the living units, to appreciate and utilize the experience and knowledge of the line-staff regarding the children. Each member of the therapeutic environment must realize his/her own unique and integral part in the growth of the child. No one person

has all the answers. Only if the team works together will the children grow;

2. Targeting specific sexual behaviors and developing a detailed intervention to modify the behavior is important. The exact verbalizations and rewards and consequences to be used should be determined, and agreed upon by all staff, before the intervention begins. As with other behavior problems, targeting specific sexual behaviors to be modified in a systematic manner brings more success than trying to change all problematic behaviors at once. When the child and staff feel success with the targeted behaviors, other sexual behaviors which require modification or cessation, can be added;

3. All staff on campus should be made aware of the behavioral interventions for children with sexual behavior problems. These childrens' sexual issues will arise with children and adults outside the living units. Substitute caregivers should be briefed on the behavioral plan before interacting with these children;

4. Open discussion of all aspects of the staff's feelings and interactions with these children. Working with children with problematic sexual behavior often stimulates very uncomfortable, sexual or punitive feelings. Interactions with these children may reawaken traumatic memories in some staff. If attention is not paid to staff reactions, a negative atmosphere for the child and the staff person can develop. It is important to be aware of any staff who is uncomfortable with children presenting such problems. Not all staff are suited to work with these children.

Prevention

As knowledge regarding the amount of mutual and forced sexual contact between young children in residential care becomes more available, it is incumbent on the institutions to develop comprehensive prevention information for children. Such a curriculum might include age-appropriate values clarification, information on natural and healthy sexuality, and how to differentiate it from coercive sexuality, and assertiveness training with role-play to stop any form of coercion. The institution's policy on physical and sexual contact between children and between children and adults should be defined and children should be made aware of the best ways to handle any problems. An open and frank discussion with all children regarding sexual behaviors in the living quarters should be ongoing.

Children Who Molest in Residential Care

The results of this study indicate that there are many children in residential care who are considered by their caregivers to have very serious sexual behavior problems. These children may force and coerce other children into sexual behaviors despite the best efforts of the staff. When a child is identified as a perpetrator of sexual abuse, the agency must assess its ability to keep the other children safe. Of course, the child's abusive behavior will be reported to the proper authorities, and precautions will be taken. While as yet unresearched, clinical information indicates that being molested by another child has very serious sequelae. This may be even more true in residential care, as the children are away from their families and may feel especially vulnerable.

It is advisable for children who molest other children to be housed together, separate from the other children. Children who molest have a myriad of problems. These children not only sexually abuse other children, they also are physically aggressive and attempt to dominate and manipulate other children in order to meet their needs. When these children are housed together, a structured, instructive, supportive, and constructive milieu, and close supervision can be provided both day and night. The major reparative work will be in the milieu, therefore staff need to be specially selected, trained and supported to work with these children. Therapy specifically focused on the sexually aggressive behaviors is essential (Gil & Johnson, 1993).

CONCLUSION AND RECOMMENDATIONS FOR FURTHER RESEARCH

One hundred and fifty-eight children between the ages of 6 and 11 in residential treatment were assessed using measures designed to study their everyday problem behaviors and their sexual behaviors. The frequency of natural and expectable sexual behaviors is given, as well as a description of more problematic sexual behaviors. The relationship between everyday problem behaviors and the children's rating on a scale to measure sexual functioning is described. The mean number of sexual behaviors of children who were both sexually and physically abused was greater than the mean number of sexual behaviors in children who were sexually abused only, but this difference was not statistically significant. The mean number of sexual behaviors of both sexually and physically abused children was significantly higher than the sexual behaviors in non-abused and physically abused children.

The data collected, as well as extensive discussion with residential staff and the authors' experience, prompted suggestions for training and supervision of child care workers and all residential staff regarding children's sexual problems.

This study demonstrated that information useful for case management, planning behavioral interventions and treatment planning can be gathered using the CSBCL and the Child Behavior Checklist. Further research might ask both child care workers and therapists to fill out the CSBCL on the same children to look at the similarities and differences in their responses. In this study there appeared to be a much higher frequency of sexual behaviors noted when therapists filled out the CSBCL, as opposed to line workers.

This study found high frequencies of children with sexual behavior problems in those residential facilities that participated. Thus, future studies should seek a random sample of residential facilities to see if this is replicated with another population. Future studies may wish to use the Group Membership Scale to ask respondents to place the children's sexual behaviors in one of the four groups from "sex play" to "perpetrating behavior." Also, further development of the CSBCL will hopefully provide weighing of certain behaviors and norms for assessing the severity of children's sexual behaviors.

NOTE

1. Arizona Children's Home Association, AZ; Beech Brook, OH; Five Acres, CA; Hillsides Episcopal Home for Children, CA; His Haven Youth Homes, CA; Northwest Children's Home, Inc., ID; Parsons Child and Family Center, NY; Parry Center, OR; Aloysius Home, RI; St. Theresa Home, TX; and The Sycamores, CA.

REFERENCES

Achenbach, T.M. (1991). *Child Behavior Checklist.* Vermont: University Associated in Psychiatry.

Finkelhor, D. (1983). Childhood sexual experiences: A retrospective survey. Unpublished manuscript. Durham, NH: University of New Hampshire.

Freud, S. (1962). *Three essays on the theory of sexuality.* New York: Basic Books.

Friedrich, W.; Grambsch, P.; Broughton D.; Kuiper, J. & Beilke, R. (1991). Normative sexual behavior in children. *Pediatrics, 88,* 556-564.

Friedrich, W.; Grambsch, P.; Damon, L.; Hewitt, S.; Koverola, C.; Lang, R.; Wolfe, V. & Broughton, D. (1992). The child sexual behavior inventory: normative and clinical comparisons. *Psychological Assessment, 4* (3), 303-311.

Gil, E. & Johnson, T.C. (1993). *Assessment and Treatment of Sexualized Children and Children who Molest.* Rockville, MD: Launch Press.

Goldman, R. and Goldman, J. (1988). *Show Me Yours–Understanding Children's Sexuality.* Penguin Books.

Haugaard, J. & Tilly, C. (1988). Characteristics predicting children's responses to sexual encounters with other children. *Child Abuse and Neglect, 12,* 209-218.

Johnson, T.C. (1991a). Children who molest: Identification and treatment approaches for children who molest other children. *The Advisor,* Fall.

Johnson, T.C. (1991b). Understanding the sexual behaviors of young children. SEICUS Report, August/September, 8-15.

Johnson, T.C. (1993). Assessment of sexual behavior problems in preschool and latency-aged children. In Yates, A. (Ed.), *Child and Adolescent Psychiatric Clinics of North America.* Philadelphia, PA: Saunders.

Johnson, T.C. (In press). Assessment of sexual behavior problems in preschool and latency-aged children. In Yates, A. (Ed.), *Child and adolescent psychiatric clinics of North America.* Philadelphia, PA: Saunders.

Dangerous Development: Considerations Concerning the Governance of Sexual Behavior in Residential Treatment Centers

Raymond Schimmer, MAT

SUMMARY. Residential treatment centers must protect residents and at the same time promote their healthy development. These duties may conflict when staff members develop policies for the government of sexual behavior of residents. Origins of this potential conflict are reviewed, and implications for policy development and practice are discussed.

Sexuality is a marvelous and precious part of an individual's existence. It opens a world of caring, human inter-relationship, and love. Sexuality is truly a wonderful thing. We have many trained staff members who can discuss it with you for hours.

The author would like to acknowledge the invaluable assistance with literature search provided by Adele Pickar, MSW, and Signia Warner, Librarian Intern. He may be written at Parsons Child and Family Center, 60 Academy Road, Albany, NY 12208.

[Haworth co-indexing entry note]: "Dangerous Development: Considerations Concerning the Governance of Sexual Behavior in Residential Treatment Centers." Schimmer, Raymond. Co-published simultaneously in *Residential Treatment for Children & Youth*, (The Haworth Press, Inc.) Vol. 11, No. 1, 1993, pp. 23-35; and: *Sexual Abuse and Residential Treatment* (ed: Wander de C. Braga, and Raymond Schimmer) The Haworth Press, Inc., 1993, pp. 23-35. Multiple copies of this article/chapter may be purchased from The Haworth Document Delivery Center. Call 1-800-3-HAWORTH (1-800-342-9678) between 9:00 - 5:00 (EST) and ask for DOCUMENT DELIVERY CENTER.

23

However, we find that we must ask you to refrain from actually doing anything remotely sexual while you are here with us at the Center. We feel kind of strongly about this, and if you could just trust us, and not do anything until discharge, we would really appreciate it. Thanks in advance for your cooperation.

Elements of the preceding apocryphal sexuality policy occasionally emerge in actual documents. Their appearance is not to be blamed on the stunted intellectual and affectual abilities of the authors, but instead upon the stress of accommodating two potentially antagonistic mandates: protecting young residents from harm while they are in care; and providing them with every opportunity for healthy growth and development.

Staff members may feel the stress most keenly when approaching the governance of actual sexual behavior. This has been, and remains, a difficult task for many reasons. We recoil instinctively from interfering in so private a function. We know comparatively little about childhood sexual behavior, and are reluctant to proceed without a fuller understanding of the phenomenon. The long-term import of childhood sexual activity may not yet be thoroughly understood (Kilpatrick, 1992), and we may be fearful of errors that can have negative implications for our residents in years to come. The behavior is by nature clandestine, and our access to it is usually limited; we often lack reliable information in specific situations. Finally, we cannot always discriminate easily between pathological and benign behavior.

These difficulties may create an institutional ambivalence that permeates a sexuality policy. Vacuous platitudes may displace substance and specificity. In the extreme case, ambivalence may prevent the development of any sort of policy, reflecting serious confusion and a consequent inability to articulate a general agency position.

Alternatively, the agency may slash the Gordian knot of complexity and develop policies frankly aimed at the prevention and elimination of all sexual activity. These policies will be highly suppressive, and may include strict segregation of residents by sex, prohibition of various male-female social activities, tight staff control over residents' friendships, vigorous procedural response to all reports of sexual behavior, careful restriction of the movement of residents, and utilization of various consequences following such activity. In theory, the behavior is eradicated, sparing both agency and residents the various afflictions that can accompany it.

The term "suppression" is not regarded here as purely pejorative. Care-taking adults naturally and usefully suppress various manifestations of behavior–much of it exploratory–on the parts of their charges. Responsible adults closely watch tree-climbing, swimming, street-crossing and sexualized play. They understand that young people are impelled to act at various points in their development well before they can appreciate the range of potential consequences. By regulating the exploratory behavior to some degree, the adult preserves the youth from errors of judgement that might damage or terminate the very development that the exploratory behavior serves to advance. This regulation usually involves a modification of the behavior, but may also on occasion require its complete prohibition. In addition to regulating exploratory behavior, residential staff members manage daily those problematic coping behaviors developed by residents prior to placement. Again, while clinical exploitation is usually preferable, there are instances in which prohibition is necessary.

There can be no question that early sexual activity–whether it be a species of developmental exploration or serious acting-out–can be highly dangerous to all participants. Residential treatment center populations are certainly vulnerable to all the generic risks of early sexual behavior, and they may well be more prone to engaging in it than are their contemporaries outside of group care. Sexually-transmitted diseases, including AIDS, currently afflict young people in increasing numbers. Early pregnancies, with all their many complications, are common. In 1985, approximately 85 of 1000 teenagers became unmarried mothers; by 1989, the number had risen to nearly 105 per 1000 (New York Times, July 26, 1992). The link between early pregnancy and poverty has been unassailably determined, and the specter of trans-generational abuse and neglect looms large in consequence.

It is likely that the type of child so often seen in residence–a survivor of less-than-optimal early care, a member of an over-stressed or fragmented family–may be one who is susceptible to engaging in sexual behavior earlier and more frequently than the general population. Benda and DiBlasio (1991), studying various theories of adolescent sexual exploration, have incorporated the often-demonstrated finding that peers affect each others' sexual activity into a broader model:

> Weak familial bonds often lead to differential association with peer groups that reinforce definitions favorable to sexual exploration because sexual engagements with peers represent a particularly intimate and immediate form of bonding. (p. 251)

Youngsters may voluntarily join peer groups that rely heavily on sexual activity to compensate for affectionate nurturance that was unavailable in their families. They may also find themselves referred to group care facilities in which the majority of their peers share similar histories and similar desires for restitutional intimacy. The likelihood of sexual activity under such circumstances may be increased.

When it does occur, sexual behavior may very well involve the abuse or exploitation of residents, many of whom begin such activity as participants, but who emerge later as traumatized victims. Unnoticed or unchecked, terribly harmful sexual activity can rage like an epidemic through facilities. Witness the cautionary tale of a pediatric psychiatric center in New York State, which can stand as an example of similar tragic episodes. In early 1987, investigators from the state's Commission on Quality of Care began examining an allegation of abuse at the center. They proceeded to unravel a skein of incidents that ultimately generated 23 allegations of sexual activity over a seven-month period. Fifteen of these involved child-child activity, of which five were ultimately proven (Commission on Quality of Care for the Mentally Disabled, 1990). Clearly, things can get out of hand. Gathering together children who have histories of abusive treatment carries serious risks for those children, and secondarily, for the staff members whose professional reputations are at stake. These risks are only justified by the potential efficacy of treatment plans, and by the ceaseless vigilance of the caregiving adults.

Finally, sexual activity of any sort among young residents presents many problems and few advantages from an administrative point of view. In addition to complex clinical and safety issues, staff members must now also deal with the law–in New York, for example, all sexual contact before age 17 is at least technically criminal–and with outside regulators, like New York's Commission on Quality of Care. All childhood sexual activity–from normative exploratory play to pathological predation–may be considered fair game for formal investigation. New words pop up in clinical and administrative discussions, such as "misdemeanor," "felony," "neglect," and "allegation," and adults begin imagining how wonderful life would be if only residents would not behave sexually. They may even dream about designing policies that could make the wish a reality.

By just "saying no," and making it stick, policy-makers can conceivably protect everyone, themselves included, while standing four-square behind the conservative dictum: "First do no harm." The chief goal of such a policy–safety–is unimpeachable. Diamond and Diamond (1986) summarize the classic argument for an active posture in a discussion of the "normative" development of pre-teens and adolescents:

> . . . the adolescents' experimental learning of sexual mores, likes, and dislikes, potentials and capabilities may be preceded by a highly sexual pre-pubertal period and follow a strongly erotic course. (p. 3)

> The authors justify intervention because the teenager's reach for independence often extracts an unfortunately high price for both the adolescent and society. (p. 3)

But despite the power of its justification and the worthiness of its aims, a "zero-tolerance" policy faces some tough contra-indications. Chief among these are the possible side-effects of guilt and shame that may be generated in youngsters as a result of environmental reaction to their sexual behavior. Allie C. Kilpatrick (1992) conducted a study of 501 middle-class women of mixed-ethnicity. She found that although the great majority of her respondents said that they had sexual experiences as children or adolescents, only 15-28% of this majority felt that the experiences were harmful. Kilpatrick's analysis of the adult functioning of her subjects leads her to believe that non-coercive, non-abusive sexual behavior may not be inexorably harmful to healthy development. Adult response to such activity, on the other hand, may be iatrogenic. Kilpatrick expresses special concern for investigations of possible abuse:

> . . . many times societal reactions to perceived abuse of children and adolescents are more harmful than the experience itself. Professionals must ensure that the results of detection, the investigation, and the agency program do not compound an already stressful situation. (p. 117)

Police-type investigations, intrusive physical examinations, and associated counseling are not entirely benign procedures. When necessary, they are invaluable; when applied in an undifferentiated manner, they can do significant harm. This is not to say directly or to imply that adults should not intervene in the sexual behavior of young residents. It is clearly their professional and legal duty to do so. However, Kilpatrick is suggesting that intervening adults act thoughtfully rather than reflexively, and that the impact of the intervention be weighed in the balance.

Moral, clinical, and legal arguments have been made against the attempted suppression of sexual behavior of residential clients. Gochros (1982), in a provocative article entitled "Social Work and the Sexual Oppression of Youth" asserts that many adults want young people to be asexual, and that they regard all youthful sexual activity as pathological. He challenges this understanding and asks:

> Might not our role as helping professionals be to permit, or even encourage the right of youth to enjoy their sexuality in non-harmful and non-exploitive contexts? (p. 44)

Gochros argues that by working to eliminate all sexual behavior, an agency may at once deprive a person of his or her right to important behavioral expression and exploration, and also fail in its duty to teach and foster development.

Stavis (1991) addressed the difficulty of being responsible for guarding both the residents' physical person, and the residents' right to behave sexually, in a discussion of three Supreme Court cases (Griswold vs. Connecticut, 1968; Youngberg vs. Romeo, 1982; Arneth vs. Gross, 1988).

A difficult dilemma arises because of the conflicting concerns in these two constitutional principles. One requires protection from exploitation or other dangers of such sexual activity, and the other affords a person the right to engage in certain sexual activity or other rights of constitutional privacy. (p. 3)

Stavis notes that the dilemma also finds expression in state and local law. One New York regulation (*State of New York Official Compilation of Codes, Rules, and Regulations, Title 14, Mental Hygiene, 633.4 (4) (XI, a,c)* for example, guarantees within a single section both a client's right to consensual activity, and the facility's right to reasonably limit the expression of sexuality.

These legal considerations are affected by several factors: age of the resident; resident's ability to consent; and the nature of local law. Clearly, an agency is not obliged to allow under-aged youth to engage in sexual behavior, but the justification for denial becomes more complicated in late adolescence. In formulating any policy, an agency must take these things into account, and should probably be prepared for a certain amount of conflict between the rights of the individual, and the rights and duties ascribed to the agency.

Stavis also offers the opinion that an agency must consider the cultural background of the resident and his/her family in making specific decisions. While an agency cannot have a separate policy for each of the large number of cultural backgrounds it serves, it can at least be clear with clients from the beginning concerning the agency's particular orientation, and about the impact its regulations may have on the individual resident.

The developmental and social forces at work in a young person's sexual existence are enormous, and a staff may easily overestimate the impact of its policies on behavior, particularly behavior that is by nature usually hidden from view. The driving forces may be irresistible, and quite immune to institutional regulation. Pre-pubertal sexual behavior, noted above by Diamond and Diamond, has been described and to some extent quantified by others as well. Hughes and Noppe (1985) cite studies from the early 1970's that estimate nearly half of all pre-adolescents engage in prolonged hugging, and that 10% female pre-teens and 28% of male pre-teens had coitus at least once. These figures compare with Kilpatrick's

(1992) finding that 55% of her sample had engaged in some type of childhood sexual activity.

Both pubertal and post-pubertal activity appears to have increased significantly in recent years and may at this point be nearly universal. Hughes and Noppe report that early 1970's studies found that about 60% of all adolescents had engaged in "heavy petting." Kilpatrick contrasts Finkelhor's 1979 finding that 66% of his subject population was sexually active through adolescence with her own recent estimate of 83%.

A complex and as yet incompletely understood interplay of biology, culture and social relationships fuels this activity. Contemporary folk lore makes much of "rampaging hormones," and there is indeed much to note. The flood of estrogens and androgens is causal in the pubertal process, and to some degree in libidinal development. Udry and Billy (1987) note that this is especially true in males, who may deal with pubertal and post-pubertal androgen levels that are 10-20 times greater than previous pre-pubertal levels. The authors may belabor the obvious when they observe: "In males, the hormone effects may overwhelm social controls" (p. 852).

These biological effects are complicated by what appears to be an astonishing acceleration in the pubertal process over the last century and a half. The average age of menarche in eight northern hemispheric industrial countries has declined from about 17.0 years in the mid-19th century, to approximately 13.0 in 1970 (Katchadourian, 1977). One might speculate that the apparent cultural acceptance and even encouragement of youthful sexual behavior is itself caused by progressively earlier physiologic development of young people (i.e., social encouragement to behave sexually begins when the society perceives that a young member is attaining physical developmental milestones).

Cultural speculation aside, there seems to be no evidence that the rate of cognitive development has accelerated similarly (Pestrak & Martin, 1985); consequently, many young people are in effect anatomical adults and psychological children. They also live within a general culture that for some reason seems to be providing progressively weaker social controls for sexual behavior. The internal inhibition is undeveloped, the external suppression is reduced, and little remains to contest the intrinsic impulse to behave sexually.

This may be a lamentable state of affairs, but the data suggests that it is also a common state of affairs. In addition to the force of what may be a cultural norm, those factors that apply particularly to youth in group care–histories of early, abusive sexual experience; association with peers who have themselves been precociously sexual; and a background of cultural and familial ambivalence regarding sexual behavior–serve almost to guarantee that youngsters will behave sexually in residence. And much of that behavior may be non-pathological, if highly problematic.

It will not do, of course, to abdicate responsibility for the governance of youthful sexual behavior on the grounds that it is now normative. Normative or not, it is still potentially devastating to growth and development. It is particularly dangerous in any sort of group treatment facility. Ignoring it, or trivializing its importance, is to court disaster on every front. Again, the New York Commission on Quality of Care (1989) report on the psychiatric center incidents may be instructive:

> In a number of cases, senior clinicians and administrators displayed an unsettling confusion or lack of understanding of the import of precocious sexual activity, including oral and anal intercourse, which were dismissed as "normal sexual experimentation" or "consensual" . . . it seems that the staff simply lost sight of the reality that these were children exhibiting troubling behaviors and needing treatment and protection. (pp. 17-18)

On the other hand, it is unlikely that agencies can fashion prelapsarian paradises of asexual youth who prepare, in complete innocence, for eventual debut into the carnal world. It is perhaps unrealistic to focus energies entirely on the prevention or suppression of behavior. Safety and protection concerning sexuality is necessary in residential care, but not entirely sufficient. Youngsters will attain menarche, will experience their first ejaculations, and will have their first interpersonal sexual experiences while in group care. They do not enter developmental hibernation on admission, however convenient that might be for all involved. The treatment center staff must accompany the youth on their developmental journeys, uncomfortable though they may be.

Kagan and Schlosberg (1989) suggest that the residential facility staff has an obligation "to recognize the youth's burgeoning sexuality and age-appropriate striving for autonomy and independence" (p. 115). Beker and Leverstein (1991) advance the notion of group care as mediator of experience for the resident. The adult, working with the resident, helps to clarify relationships between events, providing perspective on the present and connections to the past and future. In the "who am I" discussions of adolescence, one is hard-pressed to fulfill these mediating functions if simultaneously engaged in a direction that too directly refutes the biological and cultural forces at work on the resident. No one's tasks in this effort—parents, youth, or staff—are simple, but denying the complexity would seem to assure an outcome for the individual that might be less than it could have been.

CONCLUSION

The question at hand is: how far should an agency go in governing sexual behavior among its residential clients? And the answer is deceptively simple: far enough to protect, but not so far as to stifle normative development. In this, we have many problems. Our margin of error is slim, and the consequences of error are great.

There is much to be said for a strongly suppressive approach. It appears to be most conservative and therefore most responsible. But there is little reason to believe that all youthful sexual activity is harmful, and less to believe that it is all abnormal. Obviously, adult neglect of sexual behavior in residence may contribute to catastrophes of exploitation, brutality, and trauma; but excessive suppression by adults may alienate without teaching, and influence the development of long-lasting attitudes of guilt and shame. Finally, a policy that asserts something must not happen can promote the attitude that nothing does happen. This in turn may impede the development of a full, creative range of therapeutic response strategies.

If a staff chooses to attempt a style of government that balances safety and development, certain conditions must exist. The staff must be continuously aware of the nature and amount of sexual activity that occurs within a program. This awareness must include those times that residents are not directly supervised by residential staff, including school and most especially, when youth have left program without permission. Administrators must not forget that residential care is a three-shift, not a two-shift proposition. Staff members must maintain a keen sensitivity to nuance, and a willingness to uncover what may not be readily apparent, staff members cannot safely and intelligently apply differential approaches in case work.

The staff must have a reasonably reliable method of discriminating benign, exploratory, and developmentally appropriate behavior from that which is pathological and pathogenic. Being aware of particular behavior, as the New York psychiatric center staff was, is of no use if one does not understand it.

RECOMMENDATIONS

The following are recommendations for the development of treatment center sexuality policies:

1. The values and expectations of the treatment community should be clearly expressed in a sexuality policy. The individuals who comprise the adult community, beyond articulating values and expectations, must be able to explain the reasons that they hold these particular positions. (The word "inappropriate" should not appear in any such explanation.)

2. Design and implement a specific sexuality safety plan that provides for awareness of and response to a full range of resident sexual behavior. Among other things, this plan should involve a discussion of actual, specific, behaviors that staff members are likely to see, and actual, specific, responses to them. This is no place for euphemism. Masturbation, pornography, sodomy, etc., must be addressed directly.

3. Discuss the sexuality policy with families, as well as with staff and residents. There are many variations of social controls across cultures. At the least, the agency should be aware of family perspectives, and families aware of the agency's values.

4. Policies should allow for a significant measure of treatment

team autonomy in determining the cause of individual case activity. In discussing counseling strategies with adolescents, Weinstein and Rosen (1991) advocate that adults offer "a values framework that includes flexibility for autonomous, informed, decision-making" (p. 339). Similarly, a policy should offer the same flexibility to a treatment team. The team must be able to react to the needs of the individuals involved in order to assist them with their personal developmental transitions. A guiding agency policy is necessary to establish basic expectations in a potentially dangerous setting, but these limits can serve their purposes (safety and perspective) without unduly inhibiting therapeutic activity.

5. The policy should reflect concern for the residents' long-term personality development, as well as with the control of immediate sexual behavior. Twenty years ago, we may have resented external and internal scrutiny of residential sexual activity because of our concerns about the impact of such scrutiny on our treatment. Ten years ago, we may have set aside all such concerns in order to root out exploitation and abuse. We are perhaps now beginning a third phase, in which we both protect our residents from harmful sexual behavior and facilitate their growth and development in the modern world.

6. The policy should offer staff members some direction in the recognizing those behaviors likely to cause harm and differentiating them from others that may indeed be benign.

7. The agency may want to participate vigorously in state and local regulatory policy formulation. Significant variance between the agency and its funding/regulatory bodies can throw internal programs into helpless confusion, and jeopardize the agency's integrity. The subject is new, experts are few, and the involvement of those who have synthesized experience is sorely needed.

REFERENCES

Beker, J. & Feuerstein, R. (1991). The modifying environment and other environmental perspectives in group care: A conceptual contrast and integration. *Residential Treatment for Children & Youth, 8.*

Brenda, B. & DiBlasio, F. (1991). Comparison of four theories of adolescent sexual exploration. *Deviant Behavior: An Interdisciplinary Journal, 12,* 235-257.

Diamond, M. & Diamond, D. (1986). Adolescent sexuality: Biosocial aspects and intervention strategies. In Allen-Meares, P. & Shores, D. (Eds.), *Adolescent sexualities: Overviews and principles of intervention.* Binghamton, N.Y.: The Haworth Press, Inc. (pp. 3-13).

Eckholm, E. (1992, July 26). Solutions on welfare: They all cost money. *The New York Times,* pp. 1, 18.

Gochros, H. (1982). Social work and the sexual oppression of youth. *Journal of Social Work & Human Sexuality, 1,* 37-49.

Hughes, F. & Noppe, L. (1985). *Human development across the life span.* St. Paul: West Publishing.

Kagan, R. & Schlosberg, S. (1989). *Families in perpetual crisis.* New York: W.W. Norton Co.

Katchadourian, H. (1977). *The biology of adolescence.* San Francisco: W.H. Freeman and Company.

Kirkpatrick, A. (1992). *Long range effects of child and adolescent sexual experiences.* Hillsdale, New Jersey: Lawrence Erlebaum Associates, Publishers.

New York State Commission on Quality of Care for the Mentally Disabled (1990). *Investigation into allegations of child abuse and neglect at Western New York Children's Psychiatric Center: Final report.* State of New York Commission on the Quality of Care for the Mentally Disabled.

Pestrak, V. & Martin, D. (1985). Cognitive development and aspects of adolescent sexuality. *Adolescence, xx,* 981-987.

Stavis, P. (1991, November-December). Sexual activity and the laws of consent. *Quality of Care, Newsletter of the NYS Commission on Quality of Care,* p. 2.

Udry, J. & Billy, J. (1987). Initiation of coitus in early adolescence. *American Sociological Review, 52,* 841-855.

Weinstein, E. & Rosen, E. (1991). The development of adolescent sexual intimacy: Implications for counseling. *Adolescence, 26,* 331-339.

Safety Considerations in Developing an Adolescent Sex Offender Program in Residential Treatment

Jonathan E. Ross, MA
Mark P. de Villier, MSW

SUMMARY. This paper describes safety precautions utilized in the development and management of a specialized residential treatment program for adolescent sex offenders. Topics include the screening of admissions, the selection of staff and the development of a separate living unit for sex offenders. Guidelines for both resident and staff safety are presented as critical considerations in developing such a program. A strong emphasis is placed on the need for residential treatment facilities to address these safety concerns in order to enhance treatment.

Large numbers of adolescents are referred to residential treatment facilities for perpetrating child sexual abuse, forcible sexual assault, and other types of sexually aggressive behavior. With more attention being paid to this subject by judicial systems, protective

---

Please address correspondence to Jonathan Ross, MA, New Hope, Inc., 225 Midland Parkway, Summerville, SC 29485.

[Haworth co-indexing entry note]: "Safety Considerations in Developing an Adolescent Sex Offender Program in Residential Treatment." Ross, Jonathan E., and Mark P. de Villier. Co-published simultaneously in *Residential Treatment for Children & Youth*, (The Haworth Press, Inc.) Vol. 11, No. 1, 1993, pp. 37-47; and: *Sexual Abuse and Residential Treatment* (ed: Wander de C. Braga, and Raymond Schimmer) The Haworth Press, Inc., 1993, pp. 37-47. Multiple copies of this article/chapter may be purchased from The Haworth Document Delivery Center. Call 1-800-3-HAWORTH (1-800-342-9678) between 9:00 - 5:00 (EST) and ask for DOCUMENT DELIVERY CENTER.

service agencies, and the media, the number of these referrals is likely to continue increasing. There are currently over 600 specialized treatment programs in the United States that serve adolescent sex offenders, 100 of which are residential facilities (Ryan & Lane, 1991). Professionals who treat adolescents in residential care are becoming aware of the need to safely provide offender-specific services for those residents with a history of sexual aggression. New treatment approaches have emerged over the past decade with safety of the potential victim as a key concern (The National Task Force on Juvenile Sexual Offending, 1988).

The goal of such specialized residential intervention is to ultimately reduce the risk of the adolescent continuing to be sexually aggressive after discharge. An important factor in achieving this goal involves restricting the adolescent's access to potential victims until they develop internal controls for their sexually aggressive behavior. Residential treatment facilities can be excellent settings in which to assure community safety, while providing for the treatment needs of the offender. Critical issues that affect this balance are thorough admission screening procedures, careful staff selection, and intensive supervision of the residential milieu. These features must be tailored to the specific safety concerns when working with sex offenders in a residential setting.

ADMISSIONS SCREENING

Sexual offenders enter residential treatment with complex histories and treatment needs. They are not always identified upon referral as having a primary problem with sexual aggression. During the admission process, it is important to have an in-depth understanding of the characteristics of these offenders so that incidents of sexual aggression in their histories are not minimized or overlooked. Adolescent sex offenders typically have histories that include several victims, other sexually deviant "hands off" behaviors, and non-deviant sexual experiences prior to their offenses (Becker et al., 1986). Often they themselves experienced abuse and seek to satisfy deeper emotional needs such as acceptance, power, control, identification, and aggression, through sexual and criminal means (Finkelhor,

1986). Nature, extent and severity of these behaviors require careful assessment.

A specialized assessment can facilitate a decision about whether the offender's treatment needs can be met safely in a particular residential setting. For example, a sex offender with a history of running away from other placements would not be appropriate for an unlocked living unit near a family-oriented residential neighborhood. Similarly, an aggressive sex offender who committed most offenses against family members at night might not be appropriate for a dormitory setting with minimal nighttime supervision. The limitations of a residential program should be carefully considered in light of each individual's offense-specific assessment. Specialized programs have developed written guidelines to ensure consistency in determining who can be safely treated in the facility (Ross, 1991).

Some residential programs have trained specialists who complete such an assessment using comprehensive interviewing protocols (Ross & Loss, 1988). Other programs insist that a completed sex offender assessment be sent along with the usual referral information. Regardless of how assessment is completed, the referral documentation should include detailed descriptions of the adolescent's sexually aggressive behavior, existing police reports, victim's statements, protective service investigations, and incident reports from prior placements. With this information, the assessment is more likely to answer questions about the ability of the program to safely treat the referred adolescent offender. Inaccurate or incomplete assessments could lead to poor admission decisions with predictably disastrous results. An adolescent sex offender who continues to offend against others while inappropriately placed in a residential setting may become a more serious offender as a result of that placement. In such cases, the impact on victimized residents and the residential program as a whole can be devastating.

Conversely, the adolescent sex offender is entitled to the least restrictive placement that balances the needs for community and program safety as well as their own treatment needs (The National Task Force on Juvenile Sexual Offending, 1988). Many sex offenders do not require placement in a secure facility in order to benefit from specific sex offense treatment. Such offenders should not be admitted to a secure facility simply because other treatment programs are not available. Offenders who do not require secure placement may be vulnerable to other more serious offenders who do require a locked unit. The secure treatment program should be reserved for those offenders who cannot be safely treated in a less restrictive environment.

Residential treatment programs that *do not* provide specialized services for adolescent sex offenders should also be familiar with offender assessment issues. They must be able to identify and refer adolescent sex offenders to more appropriate programs if they cannot provide offender-specific services in safe environments. Residential programs should take advantage of the numerous training opportunities available focusing on interviewing and assessing the adolescent sex offender. Sex offender assessment has become so specialized that one state has already enacted legislation to separately license these professionals (The Legislature of the State of Washington, 1990). Unfortunately, many general residential programs continue to accept offenders who end up abusing other residents while in placement, only later referring them for specialized treatment.

STAFF SELECTION

The screening, training and supervision of direct care staff who work with the offenders is also a key safety consideration. It is important to screen potential employees in a systematic way to minimize the possibility of hiring persons with histories of sexual aggression. Adolescent offenders may be particularly vulnerable to abusive staff members due to their histories of victimization and their diminished public credibility. A structured screening protocol (Loss, 1987), criminal history search, protective service search and thorough reference check are vital components of employee screening. Although there is no reliable way to identify a sex offender other than by criminal history, thorough screening procedures can act as a strong deterrent. Once hired, every staff member should read and sign a comprehensive policy on how allegations of staff abuse are investigated, validated, and resolved. Creating an atmosphere where these procedures are openly discussed may be a further deterrent to a potentially abusive employee.

It is important to select mature direct care staff members who are self-confident, comfortable with sexual issues, non-judgmental, and not easily intimidated by adolescents. There may be instances where an aggressive sex offender attempts to make a particular staff member feel afraid of being sexually assaulted by that resident. If that staff member appears outwardly fearful of the offender, there is a greater potential for the latter to perceive the former as vulnerable, rendering the staff member a potential target for aggression. An effective staff member establishes firm personal boundaries and believes in his or her ability to control the residential milieu even when personally challenged by offenders. Accepting these challenges without feeling attacked, or becoming aggressive, or harshly judging offenders will reinforce safe boundaries between staff members and residents.

Staff members are also expected to be involved in explicit discussions about sexual aggression on a regular basis as part of the offender's treatment. Finally, there will be times when staff members are the target of the offenders' deviant sexual fantasies. In all of these instances, staff members cannot show excessive vulnerability, fear, or embarrassment. To do so might inadvertently encourage offenders to become inappropriate and to escalate their behaviors to a point such that staff safety is threatened.

Attention should also be paid to the possibility that initial contact with identified sex offenders may bring up personal issues for a new staff member. Staff struggling with unresolved victimization, family dysfunction or sexually deviant impulses of their own may react in a destructive manner when working with this population. Supervisory personnel should watch for excessive anger, identification, punitive limit-setting and inappropriate self-disclosure. Each of these reactions could create unsafe situations in the treatment milieu. For example, a female staff member with her own unresolved feelings of sexual victimization may show intense anger towards the offenders and become a target for sexual assault by an aggressive offender who perceives her anger as a personal attack. Preparatory training on personal issues that may arise when working with this population should be mandatory; regular and structured clinical supervision sessions for direct care staff is also essential.

SUPERVISING THE TREATMENT MILIEU

The Living Unit

Ideally, sex offenders should be housed separately from those residents without a history of sexual aggression. The safety and treatment benefits of the specialized milieu seem to far outweigh the difficulties that arise when "labeling" of the separate living unit occurs. It is usually possible to prevent other residents from harassing residents in the identified offender unit by having a strong educational program on sexual aggression. All staff members and residents should be presented with information dispelling the myths about sexual abuse, sex offenders and specialized treatment. Educational videotapes have been recently developed which can assist in this process (Bellefaire, 1990). The sex offender treatment staff can then present an overview of the program without discussing specific resident's histories. A policy prohibiting harassment between living units should be established and strictly enforced by staff in an open and direct manner. The separate unit for sex offenders will then be able to provide specific treatment activities, specialized supervision, and an open atmosphere in which to discuss sexual issues.

There may be times when a facility must care for sex offenders in living units for non-offender residents. For example, a resident may be identified as a sex offender only after placement in a residential facility where treatment for other clinical issues has been initiated. In such cases the sex offender should be placed with other residents who have similar general diagnoses, and histories of similar non-sexual dysfunctional behavior. For example, conduct disordered residents with histories of antisocial behavior would be less vulnerable to victimization by an aggressive sex offender. Residents who are passive, depressed, prone to isolation or who function at a lower intellectual level may be particularly vulnerable to the sex offender. Residents who are placed in residential treatment primarily to address their own victimization, especially those who are experiencing Post Traumatic Stress Disorder, should *never* be placed in living units with sex offenders, as they would be easy targets for exploitation by the sex offender.

Programs with mixed populations may be tempted to keep the existence of sex offender services secret in hopes of avoiding the "labeling" effect. This approach can create serious problems. First, a majority of offenders have victimized and been victimized in secrecy (Finkelhor, 1986). Denial, dishonesty, minimization and cognitive distortion are common ways for offenders to avoid detection and reduce internal conflict. Some cognitive distortions even serve to support the offender's "cycle" of sexually aggressive behavior (Becker et al., 1989; Abel & Blanchard, 1974). A treatment milieu that avoids dealing openly with the offender's history could potentially reinforce this already strong tendency towards secrecy and distortion. Second, it is inevitable that non-offender residents will find out about the existence of sex offender treatment within the facility. When this happens in a manner that is not initiated and controlled by staff, then harassment of the sex offenders is likely to develop and remain secret. Finally, an atmosphere of secrecy could make it easier for an offender to exploit a non-offender resident.

It is important to consider the offender's access to potential victims who visit the residential program. Pre-adolescent children should never be allowed in an area where they might have unsupervised contact with offenders. Many programs allow only visits by the immediate family members who were not victimized by the offender. These visits should be carefully supervised so that the offender has little opportunity to behave in a sexually inappropriate manner. Family members should be clearly informed of these restrictions prior to admission to the residential facility.

Resident Safety

Even within a living unit that houses only sex offenders, there is always potential for sexual exploitation. Attention should be paid to the makeup of the living unit to avoid extreme differences in physical size, age, social skills, intellectual functioning and severity of offending behavior. Single rooms are the ideal solution for a sex offender living unit. If single rooms are not available, offenders should be placed together in sleeping quarters with other offenders who are similar diagnostically and behaviorally. The night shift must include awake staff who make frequent bed checks to ensure that there is little opportunity for sexual abuse. These checks must occur randomly, never following a pattern that the offenders can predict.

In general, visual supervision of the offenders should be as thorough as possible. Special guidelines should be established for the supervision of bedrooms, rest rooms and shower areas. Where semi-private rooms are utilized, roommates should never be allowed to close their bedroom doors unless they are alone. Dormitory-style living areas should be arranged to allow for a safe distance between beds and dressing areas. Bunk beds are not recommended unless staff members are physically present and awake *inside* the dormitory unit at all times during the night shift.

Rest rooms and showers should be used by one offender at a time, if possible, or in a staggered fashion so that offenders are not entering or exiting at the same time. Offenders should be required to be fully covered when entering or leaving these areas to minimize opportunities for exhibitionism. Staff members should be trained to closely supervise these areas without placing themselves in a position such that they can easily see undressed offenders.

Staff should be aware of how and with whom offenders develop friendships in the living unit. Appropriate friendships between offenders of similar age, social skills, and developmental level should be encouraged. Friendships that might negatively affect a less disturbed, younger, or more vulnerable offender should be discouraged. Food, clothing and any personal items should never be exchanged between offenders without staff scrutiny; offenders often manipulate these transactions to bribe or intimidate potential victims.

When sexual exploitation is suspected or does occur in the living unit, the incident should be investigated immediately with separate interviews of the residents involved. The interviewer should be non-judgmental in tone but insistent upon the details of the incident. Interviewers should establish who initiated the contact, if there were promises or threats made, how long it has been occurring, whether there was any physical force or intimidation used, and whether there was verbal consent. Staff members should remember that verbal consent does not necessarily mean that the incident was not abusive, because bribery may have occurred. The residents involved in the incident should remain separated until its resolution to prevent the possibility that threats by an offender may intimidate another into secrecy. Outward signs of these threats usually appear in the form of menacing looks and rumors among other offenders.

If the particular incident is clearly found to be a sexual assault involving force, intimidation, or coercion, the responsible offender should be charged criminally since accountability is an important part of intervention (The National Task Force on Juvenile Sexual Offending, 1988). If possible, the offender should be removed from the living unit for the safety of the other residents. If the incident is found to be generally abusive but not technically criminal, the responsible offender should be given the appropriate consequences within the program. If possible, the offender should be removed from the living unit until he/she takes responsibility for the incident and genuinely apologizes to the other resident. In either case, staff supervision and resident sleeping arrangements should be adjusted to prevent further incidents.

Adolescent sex offenders can be sexually inappropriate in ways that are indirect, clever, brief, and difficult to observe. For example, an offender may become sexually aroused after purposely brushing up against another resident or staff member, while insisting that the contact was accidental. Hallways, doorways and corners are particular areas where offenders may engage in this behavior. The program should emphasize at all times the importance for offenders to maintain appropriate personal distance from each other and staff. For this reason, physical displays of affection such as hugs should not be permitted in a sex offender program. Handshakes and pats on the shoulder are permissible as manners of greeting others which maintain appropriate personal distance.

When many offenders are together in a contained common area such as a day room, it is important to deploy staff on all sides of the area to maximize observation. Some staff members should remain standing facing the residents, and moving throughout the area. This procedure enhances the safety of the unit by maximizing staff's observation of offender's hands and genital areas. Offenders should not be allowed to lie down in common areas of the unit as some will use this position to engage in sexually inappropriate behaviors. When lining up offenders to move through the facility, staff should be deployed at points along the line, not just at the front and rear. Offenders may use this situation to "bump" into other residents.

Some programs are completely self-contained, but others have sex offenders living in a separate unit while participating in the mainstream of activities with other residents in the facility. It is important to pay even closer attention to resident supervision whenever the sex offenders have contact with non-offending residents. Offenders should be carefully monitored for any sexually inappropriate gestures or verbal comments during these activities and while in transit to other parts of the facility. Contact between offender and non-offender populations should be especially avoided during unstructured free time.

Staff Safety

There are sex offenders who may pose a threat to residential staff. A staff member should never be placed alone in an isolated area with one or several offenders with histories of sexual assault against peers or older victims. Special attention should also be paid when transporting this type of offender to places outside the facility. Staffing patterns should be adjusted to ensure that no individual staff member is left in a vulnerable situation. Staff members should remain within sight of each other. They should not enter a bedroom, rest room or shower area without a colleague "covering" them. Two-way radios are strongly recommended for staff communication. When offenders do act in a sexually inappropriate manner towards staff members, the former should be confronted immediately in an even tone and consequences should be imposed when necessary.

The program should ensure that personal information about staff members, such as their home address or phone number, is not kept in any place accessible to a sex offender. Magazine subscriptions with home address labels seem to be a common source for this information. Of course, staff members are discouraged from directly disclosing any such personal information to the offenders. Particular attention must be paid to avoid unwitting disclosures when staff members talk to each other in situations where an offender might overhear it. Manipulative sex offenders who have been in residential care for long periods of time can become skilled at listening to staff conversations while appearing to attend to something else.

In addition to these specific safety considerations, staff members should keep in mind that the more structured and effective the clinical treatment program, the lower the likelihood that resident and staff safety will be jeopardized. Focused residential treatment can teach offenders to control their behavior, but successful outcome depends on the establishment and maintenance of a safe environment for all involved.

REFERENCES

Abel, G. & Blanchard, E. (1974). The role of fantasy in the treatment of sexual deviation. *Archives of General Psychiatry, 30*, 467-75.

Becker, J.B.; Cunningham-Rathner, J. & Kaplan, M.F. (1986). Adolescent sexual offenders: Demographics, criminal sexual histories, and recommendations for reducing future offenses. *Journal of Interpersonal Violence*, (4), 431-45.

Bellefaire/Jewish Children's Bureau (1990). Breaking the cycle: Adolescent sexual offenders. Video available from Producers: P.O. Box 18009, Cleveland, OH 44118-0009.

Finkelhor, D. (1986). *A source book on child sexual abuse.* Beverly Hills, CA: Sage Publications.

The Legislature of the State of Washington (1990). Second Substitute Senate Bill No. 6259, Chapter 3, Laws of 1990, 51st Legislature Regular Session.

Loss, P. (1987). Big Brother, Big Sister of Worcester County: Interview/screening guidelines. Available from Big Brothers, Big Sisters of Worcester County, Inc., 50 Franklin Street, Suite 10, Worcester, MA 01608.

The National Task Force on Juvenile Sexual Offending (1988). Preliminary report from the National Task Force on juvenile sexual offending. *Juvenile and Family Court Journal, 39* (2), 5-67.

Ross, J.E. (1991). Making recommendations for sex offending clients: Abbreviated risk levels and areas. Training workshop handout available from author: P.O. Box 428, Mt. Pleasant, SC 29465.

Ross, J.E. & Loss, P. (1988). Risk assessment/interviewing protocol for adolescent sex offenders. Available from author: P.O. Box 428, Mt. Pleasant, SC 29465.

Ryan, G. & Lane, S. (1991). *Juvenile sexual offending: Causes, consequences, and corrections.* Lexington, MA: Lexington Books.

Ensuring That All Children and Adolescents in Residential Treatment Live in a Protected, Safe Environment

Beth Caldwell, MS
Erlinda Rejino, MS

SUMMARY. A large number of children come to residential treatment with histories of sexual abuse. These children often unknowing-
ly make themselves vulnerable to future victimization or else sexually
abuse other children. It is the responsibility of the residential program
administration to protect all children in their care. Ensuring this
protection is not an abstract concept. Definite changes in administrative, clinical, and direct care practices can ensure a safe environment.
This article identifies safety factors and describes policies and practices found to be effective in establishing a safe environment.

Correspondence may be addressed to either author at the New York State
Office of Mental Health, Bureau of Children and Families, 44 Holland Avenue,
Albany, NY 12229.

[Haworth co-indexing entry note]: "Ensuring That All Children and Adolescents in Residential Treatment Live in a Protected, Safe Environment." Caldwell,
Beth, and Erlinda Rejino. Co-published simultaneously in *Residential Treatment
for Children & Youth*, (The Haworth Press, Inc.) Vol. 11, No. 1, 1993, pp. 49-62;
and: *Sexual Abuse and Residential Treatment* (ed: Wander de C. Braga, and
Raymond Schimmer) The Haworth Press, Inc., 1993, pp. 49-62. Multiple copies
of this article/chapter may be purchased from The Haworth Document Delivery
Center. Call 1-800-3-HAWORTH (1-800-342-9678) between 9:00 -5:00 (EST)
and ask for DOCUMENT DELIVERY CENTER.

49

INTRODUCTION

The literature on the effectiveness of residential treatment is sparse (Wells, 1991). When a child or adolescent[1] enters any type of residential treatment, it is hoped that certain goals will be achieved. Child-specific goals include:

1. the child will reside in a protected, safe environment;
2. the child will live amidst warmth, love, support and kindness;
3. the child will, through the therapeutic milieu and other specific treatment interventions, heal, grow strong, learn new skills, identify and solve problems that have caused him/her pain or difficulties, and be ready to function successfully at home, in a less restrictive home-like setting, or independent living environment.

Although administrative staff of all residential programs devote time, energy and staff training resources to ensure the achievement of these goals, there has been a lack of attention to comprehensively defining what are the components of a protective and safe environment, and how to achieve them. This lack of attention, combined with the large number of children in residential care who have histories of sexual abuse, has resulted in children in our care often being allowed to engage in child to child sexual activity, in detriment to their treatment goals.

Without clear definitions, administrative and clinical practices have, often "in the name of treatment," denied children needed protection (Small et al., 1991). This unfortunate circumstance has not been intentional, rather administrators and clinicians often have not been aware of the sexual histories of the children in their care, have not been aware of their impact on child to child sexual activity, and have not known how to protect them. Administrators and clinicians have focused on other treatment needs, unaware that the children's sexual activity could preclude the achievement of a safe environment. Ironically, while administrators and clinicians can ensure that children are kept safe, they often cannot predict the outcome of milieu and treatment interventions (Curry, 1991).

---

1. Hereafter referred to as child or children.

Examples of administrative and clinical practices that preclude safety are numerous:

1. A psychiatrist kept a child's history of sexual perpetration out of the referral material to ensure admittance to a foster home. The child later sexually abused the natural and other foster children in the family. Had this entire family been educated about practices to safeguard against sexual abuse, the referred child could have entered the foster home and remained there successfully;

2. The treatment team (including an administrator, a social worker, a psychiatrist and a child care worker) from a residential program disputed an outside reviewer's recommendation that bedroom doors be locked when not in use, and that children should have to ask permission to enter their bedrooms. Despite the large number of children with identified histories of sexual abuse and subsequent sexual activity, the team strongly believed that the children needed to feel "at home." Many of the children in this program subsequently experienced sexual victimization in their bedrooms, much as they had experienced earlier at home;

3. Administrators in a residential program were reluctant to implement a recommendation made by outside reviewers for staff to conduct 15-minute variable checks on each resident with flashlights (during late evening and night shifts). Child care staff felt that this was intrusive, children complained that the flashlights would wake them up, clinical staff felt that this would provoke stress in the team, and administrative staff felt that they needed to support staff and respect the children's concerns. The latter, of course, could voice complaints about the flashlights but couldn't complain about the subsequent molestations by other children for fear of reprisal;

4. Reviewers found that staff were not conducting comprehensive and structured change of shift meetings every day and every shift to relay crucial information about the children (especially important to staff new to the unit). Both an executive director and a program coordinator insisted, in response to recommendations based on such findings, that the reviewers were wrong, and that the shift meetings that did occur were sufficient. They also emphasized the effectiveness of the existing weekly treatment team meeting in accomplishing the goal of communicating important information. These administrators spent a great deal of energy rejecting the critical

feedback, but too little in reviewing and improving upon existing procedures. A child with an identified history of sexual perpetration (a fact unknown to new staff) was able to obtain permission to use a bathroom while unsupervised and call forth three different boys, one after another, to perform sexual acts on him.

The list of examples illustrating administrative and clinical practices that preclude safety is endless. Nonetheless, it is encouraging to find that many administrators have more recently begun to review their objectives and priorities. They came to understand that a safe environment represents a foundation without which a caring and therapeutic environment cannot be built.

The New York State Office of Mental Health (OMH) learned about the importance of this foundation in mid-1988. Then, several children in one of its state-operated children's inpatient programs were found to have been involved in sexual activities with each other on a number of occasions. OMH subsequently reviewed and identified factors that contributed to these events and developed a protocol with which to review the other 14 state-operated children's inpatient programs. In addition, OMH found that the identified problematic factors were not hospital-specific, but represented systemic issues needing correction. Subsequent reviews of residential treatment facilities, private hospitals, and group home programs confirmed that indeed these were not hospital-specific factors, but systemic problems that could make any residential program vulnerable to unsafe child to child sexual activity.

CRITICAL FACTORS FOR A SAFE ENVIRONMENT

The Office of Mental Health identified five factors critical to keeping children safe from sexual activity in a residential setting:

  I.   Administrative understanding and commitment.
 II.   Environmental factors.
III.   Staff attitudes.
 IV.   Clinical factors.
  V.   The investigatory and incident review processes.

OMH broke down each area into a checklist which provides a mechanism for programs to evaluate their ability to protect children from child to child sexual activity, and to ensure proper care and treatment for children with histories of sexual abuse. Examples of expanded checklists for factors II and V can be found in the addenda. Checklists for all five factors are available from the authors; an overview of these follows.

Critical Factor I: Administrative Understanding and Commitment

Underlying the other four factors, there *must* be an administrative understanding of, and commitment to, establishing safe practices. OMH found that the number of in-hospital child sexual incidents correlated inversely with the commitment of the administrative staff to making vigorous changes in policy and practice. Administrators who made excuses and rationalized that safety measures could not be implemented, or could only partially be implemented, continued to put their children at risk for sexual victimization by other children. Administrators who vigorously evaluated the other four factors in their programs and implemented comprehensive changes recognized immediate results. This was confirmed later by a comprehensive outside review process, by child interviews, and by the fact that sexual incidents involving children were virtually eliminated.

Critical Factor II: Environmental Factors

Environmental factors impacting on safety include physical plant, child supervision protocols, daily routines, child feedback mechanisms, and degree of administrative presence. Regardless of program size–be it a group home with four beds or a large congregate care campus setting–these environmental factors must be carefully reviewed, and specific procedures developed, so that a protected environment can be attained.

A review of the program's *physical plant* is critical. This review should identify the need to reconfigure physical space to allow for small group activities; to provide for a sufficient number of single bedrooms and small, easily supervised, bathrooms; and to close up or secure open spaces which pose supervision problems. Often physical plant considerations directly affect child supervision protocols. For example, well placed supervision posts are crucial in that they allow staff to view all open hallways from a central position. *Child supervision protocols* focus staff attention on the need to be consistently vigilant in the supervision of their charges. These protocols should clearly address several areas such as evening and night rounds, unsupervised or unescorted time, and individual usage of bedrooms and bathrooms. *Daily routines* which incorporate informative change of shift meetings, attention to specific supervisory needs during transition times, activities for free time planned in advance and offering a wide variety of programs, and frequent community meetings, all provide a structure which encourages staff to focus on child safety.

The last two environmental factors include opportunity for *children to give feedback* about their care and treatment and an *administrative presence* which models quality interactions and monitors program implementation. A specific checklist for these environmental factors is available in Addendum 1.

Critical Factor III: Staff Attitudes

In order to ensure the safety of children in residential programs, it is crucial that honest and consistent communication occurs between all child-related environments, including residential, clinical, educational, recreational and home. Those in charge of each environment must understand the importance of a vigilant attitude toward safety. Although it is not possible to dictate attitudes via policies and procedures, it is possible to define expectations and behaviors sufficiently to influence attitudes. Staff attitudes, as a critical factor in ensuring a safe environment, incorporate three main areas:

- Clear articulation of an overall *program philosophy;*
- *Clinical leadership*;
- *Staff awareness and training.*

The *program philosophy* should address sexuality as a developmental process and should emphasize that the history of sexual abuse/activity is a reality for many children. Clear definitions for acceptable and unacceptable resident behaviors, particularly sexual behaviors, should be included in the program philosophy. It should stress concern for child safety and sensitivity in the handling of sexual incidents. Promoting comfort levels when exchanging important information with family or respite providers must also be an important emphasis.

The *clinical leadership* of the program has many responsibilities related to safety. Leaders should be well versed in the treatment of child sexual abuse and general child development, especially as related to sexual issues. They must take an active role in developing and implementing a treatment philosophy and be vigilant in supervising all aspects of treatment–from assessment, to choice of treatment modalities, to discharge planning–to ensure appropriate and comprehensive attention to sexual issues.

Clinical leaders must ensure competent clinical consultation to staff for whom the topic of sexual abuse brings forth their own histories, cultural differences, and fears. It is also their responsibility to oversee the provision of staff training and supervision in the areas of sexual development and sexual abuse. Provision of child and parent orientation, ongoing education about sexuality and practices to ensure safety, reporting of incidents and concerns in the milieu, as well as behavioral expectations for children, are additional tasks that leaders must address.

In the area of *staff awareness and training,* topics covered must include safe child supervision practices, clinical issues associated with sexual abuse, and methods of working with children who have been sexually abused.

Critical Factor IV: Clinical Factors

The clinical area is heavily influenced by the philosophical stance of the agency and the attitudes supported by that philosophy. Agencies featuring a pro-active posture in pursuing information on sexual issues and documenting it are more apt to have a clearly defined plan to deal with potential problems. Key components of the clinical documentation section include sexual history, treatment issues, discharge planning, special precautions, and needed expertise from clinical staff.

Programs should *actively* seek a sexual history. Documentation of sexual development and history should be included in all assessments (e.g., nursing, psychiatric, social work). Programs should also ensure that each historical finding of abuse, or suspicion of abuse, results in a recommendation for treatment or documentation as to why treatment is not appropriate at the time. Addressing sexual issues in a treatment plan must go beyond the control of sexual behaviors. The underlying dynamic issues contributing to the acting out behaviors must be addressed to facilitate healing.

Probably one of the areas least considered and relative to identified sexual history and/or incidents is *discharge planning.* Yet, lack of attention to sexual history and incidents when discharge plans are implemented has resulted in numerous child to child sexual events. Discharge plans should include attention to sexual history and incidents, as well as child, parent, and staff needs (i.e., training, education, treatment and precautions) in the child's post-discharge living environment.

Crucial to the safety of any residential program is the development and implementation of individualized precautions based on each child's history, symptomatology and behavior. Any additional supervision or supports needed must be indicated in the treatment plan and shared with all staff. It is highly recommended that programs ensure that *special precautions,* as related to sexuality, be reviewed in each change of shift meeting, similarly to existing practices concerning suicide risk management. Special precautions may include assignment to a single bedroom, a bedroom close to a staff post, or a certain mix of children in a bedroom; one-to-one supervision all of the time or during certain group or escort times; caution in scheduling male or female staff for singular escort; singular use of bathroom, etc.

Finally, each agency should establish *clinical criteria* for all of those working with sexually abused children. Training and supervision should occur until such criteria are met.

Critical Factor V: Investigatory and Incident Review Processes

Proper investigation and incident review ensure that accurate reporting of untoward incidents does occur, that emergency policies and procedures are implemented, and that immediate safety needs of residents receive attention. The review process also helps evaluate the nature of the incident, thus providing information that may help prevent future occurrences. Policies and procedures for the investigatory and review processes should address three areas: definition of reportable incidents and outline of subsequent investigatory routines; procedures for handling matters of safety, clinical, and medical import following an incident or allegation; and systematic review of incidents plus implementation of recommendations. A specific checklist for this factor is provided in Addendum 2.

CONCLUSION

Our experience indicates that the provision of a residential environment safe from sexual exploitation and abuse correlates with the ability of staff, clinical and administrative, to review, re-think, and introduce changes in various critical areas as described above. Administrative commitment to change is of the essence; energy, enthusiasm, consistency and on-site presence are additional requirements, if changes are to occur in an enduring fashion. Once fully implemented, the added structure and protection are likely to be welcomed by children and staff alike. Children will feel safer, and staff members will feel better able to provide protection not only for their charges but for themselves, as the potential for unwanted incidents and allegations is reduced. The first and fundamental goal of ensuring that each child resides in a protected, safe environment, is attainable. Once each child is safeguarded, the therapeutic program can focus on other goals that enable a true healing process.

REFERENCES

Curry, J. (1991). Outcome research on residential treatment: Implementations and suggested directions. *American Journal of Orthopsychiatry, 63* (37), 348-356.

Small, R.; Kennedy, K. & Bender, B. (1991). Critical issues for practice in residential treatment: The view from within. *American Journal of Orthopsychiatry, 63,* (3), 327-338.

Wells, K. (1991). Long-term residential treatment for children: Introduction. *American Journal of Orthopsychiatry, 61* (3), 324-326.

ADDENDUM 1

Environmental Factors Checklist

A. Physical Plant Considerations

Issues to consider that may require plant changes:

1. Is there a sufficient number of single bedrooms? For ideal supervision all children should have single bedrooms. There should be no bedrooms with more than two beds.
2. Is there a sufficient number of small bathrooms? Ideally children should *only* use the bathroom *one* at a time.
3. Is the space configured so that no more than 6-8 children are programmed in a defined space? If census demands numbers higher than these, can it be reduced or can space be reconfigured?
4. Are all living and program spaces clearly marked off and easily closed off? All open hallways or spaces should be visible to the staff from a central post in the residence.
5. Are there proper locks on bedroom, bathroom, closet and program area doors (i.e., can be opened from inside, but not from the outside without a key)?
6. Are the spaces separating programs (e.g., school and residence) secure?

B. Child Supervision Protocols

Issues to consider that may require changes in policies, procedures and/or practices.

1. Are there policies governing how many children can use the bathroom at a time; whether bathrooms must be locked when not in use?
2. Are there policies governing bedroom usage? Can bedroom doors be closed when more than one child is in the bedroom? If so, under what conditions?
3. Are there specific criteria allowing children to have unsupervised or unescorted time? Sexual histories should be a determining factor. It is always best to err conservatively. For children needing escorts, are the escort procedures consistent and comprehensive?

4. Are staff deployed to provide optimum visual supervision? Do they have posts? Was the physical layout considered in establishing the posts?
5. Are there transportation procedures indicating where staff members sit in vehicles to provide maximum supervision and ensure safety?
6. Is there a clearly defined procedure for staff to check on residents throughout the day and evening? Are time lines, protocols and documentation needs clearly indicated?
7. Policies and procedures for late evening checks and night rounds should address each of the following areas:

   - no more than 15 minutes between resident checks;
   - variably scheduled checks;
   - clear definition of how to check (i.e., use a flashlight, enter the room, see the child);
   - clear documentation of rounds;
   - specific protocols for other night tasks to ensure that they do not interfere with rounds;
   - documented frequent random supervisory checks to ensure consistent implementation of all procedures noted above.

8. Is there planned supervision for visiting community friends?

C. Daily Routines

1. Structured shift change meetings for all shifts, to ensure consistent exchange of information. Shift meeting procedures should address or include:

   - length: one-half hour recommended;
   - presence of previous shift supervisor;
   - regular clinical staff involvement; and
   - an agenda which covers special supervision and/or precaution issues, posting and escorting responsibilities, noteworthy incidents from previous shift, and potential concerns.

2. Are evening and weekend recreation programs structured, planned well in advance, and do they feature variety?
3. Is there a plan for difficult-to-manage transition times (i.e., after school, after supper, before bed)? Increase the presence of staff during transition times and/or use short periods of quiet or study time between activities.

D. Protocols to Ensure That Residents Are Encouraged to Report Uncomfortable, Unpleasant, or Abusive Interactions

1. Are there structured daily individual meetings with each child which include time for the child to share concerns and complaints?
2. Are there daily and structured family or community meetings?
3. Are child consumer evaluations conducted twice yearly by non-program staff?

E. Administrative and Clinical Presence on Residential Unit

1. Are there announced and unannounced administrative rounds that ensure consistent implementation of policies and procedures?
2. Is there a regular clinical presence to model quality interactions, to lead therapy groups, and to be involved in other aspects of the program?

ADDENDUM 2

Investigation and Incident Review Process Checklist

A. Prior to a Sexual Incident, Ensure:

- There are clear definitions of reportable incidents congruent with laws and regulations; (This is vital to helping staff identify the types of incidents they should report).
- There is an established and clear investigatory routine for those incidents requiring investigation.
- There is a roster of specially trained investigators.
- Service agreements exist with specialized medical clinics and local law enforcement agencies.

B. Immediately After an Alleged Sexual Incident, Ensure:

- The safety of children involved in incident (i.e., separating children, keeping child in presence of a staff member).
- Sensitivity on the part of staff members handling the incident.
- Proper medical follow-up.
- Clear, concise and appropriate incident documentation.
- Commencement of a proper type of investigation.
- Immediate clinical support (as well as evaluation of future clinical needs).
- Issuance of special supervision or precautions for child(ren) involved.
- Review and possible modification of treatment plan (or documentation of the rationale for no change).
- Consideration of the need for immediate or long-term changes in administrative supervision practices, training requirements, communication avenues, activity schedules, child supervision, or staff supervisory practices.
- Proper notifications of parents, law enforcement and others as required.
- Openness and clarity in sharing information about alleged sexual activities with other children.

C. Review of All Incidents

The policies and procedures in this area are vitally important in identifying and correcting systemic issues affecting safety. Areas which must be clearly addressed in this area include:

1. Minutes of Review Meetings–The items included in the minutes should be clearly outlined and include statistical information to analyze trends, as well as follow-up information on incident.
2. Monitoring mechanism–Each agency should have a mechanism in place to monitor the implementation of all recommendations generated through the incident review process.
3. Review chair–It is important that the objectivity of this review mechanism be guarded. The chair of this committee should not be the program director, if that person is

involved in the investigation or other aspects of the review process.

4. Identification and protection of children who are the subjects of repeated allegations–a comprehensive mechanism must exist to identify children/staff who are involved in more than one incident, who make more than one allegation, or who are the target of more than one allegation. The mechanism must include comprehensive follow-up of "repeat" incidents–specifying treatment changes, supervision changes, staff training or other interventions–so that effectiveness can be assessed.

Staff Training Needs Around Sex Abuse in Residential Treatment

David A. Nevin, PhD

SUMMARY. Residential centers have been largely reactive to critical incidents and outside regulators in response to concerns around
sexual abuse. Yet residential centers have the resources to become
leaders in the field of sex abuse prevention and treatment. A large
number of victims and potential offenders are in residential placement. The challenge of providing a safe milieu and a healing environment, enthusiastic staff and experience give residences an edge.
A matrix with four levels of staff training is presented along with
some special needs of staff at each level of involvement in sex abuse
work. The article suggests that staff preparedness would let residential settings take the lead in the field of sex abuse treatment.

He's 20. He's one week into his new job as a child care worker.
He's working the evening shift in a residential setting for adolescent
girls. His senior co-worker, being female, is helping the girls in the
shower room. He's in the dorm's corridor seeing that the girls get
into their rooms and stay there.

Already one of the girls has come out of her room clad only in

Dr. Nevin may be written at the following address: Center for Human Growth,
550 Washington Avenue, Albany, NY 12203.

[Haworth co-indexing entry note]: "Staff Training Needs Around Sex Abuse
in Residential Treatment." Nevin, David A. Co-published simultaneously in *Residential Treatment for Children & Youth*, (The Haworth Press, Inc.) Vol. 11, No. 1,
1993, pp. 63-80; and: *Sexual Abuse and Residential Treatment* (ed: Wander de C.
Braga, and Raymond Schimmer) The Haworth Press, Inc., 1993, pp. 63-80. Multiple copies of this article/chapter may be purchased from The Haworth Document Delivery Center. Call (1-800-342-9678) between 9:00 - 5:00 (EST) and ask
for DOCUMENT DELIVERY CENTER.

63

her Levis and bra, one strap off the shoulder, asking him with a smile if he can come into her room and talk since, "You're the only staff who I feel close to." It crossed his mind to slide the strap up to her shoulder. Now he hears a 13-year old crying in her bed. He asks her what the trouble is. Lying on her face, she continues to sob and strike her fists against the mattress. He asks again, "What's wrong?" Through the sobs she asks him, "Why did my daddy make me do those things?"

Is he ready for all this?

STAFF PREPAREDNESS–AN OVERVIEW

Staff "Preparedness"–Compliance or Pro-active? Child abuse, both physical and sexual, is of special import in residential placement since a disproportionate number of abuse victims and emerging offenders are brought together in these settings. Krenk (1984) reports 69% of the girls and 50% of the boys at the Christie school had a documented history of inappropriate sexual contact with an adult. Rindfleisch and Rabb (1984) suggest that residential reports are twice those of family reports. This means that the children in placement have had twice as much exposure to abusive experiences sometime in their lives.

Many children are in residence for their protection since placement is one form of protective custody. Some are there because they abused. Many have abuse issues when placement occurs for other problems like truancy, running, or the popular "ungovernability"! Oles (1991) says that 70% of residents in his experience were abused. Yet he laments that residential programs have been primarily custodial, leaving the treatment of abuse to outpatient settings. "As a result, the role the cottage program and the child care worker can play in helping these youth has not been adequately elaborated" (Ibid., p. 44).

How prepared are our residential staffs to deal with such an important issue for so many of the residents? Agency preparedness has followed the pattern of response to abuse that emerged in our society. Essentially ignored until the 50s and 60s, concern was raised by a few individuals but was ignored by the mainstream. It was Kempe's "The Battered Child Syndrome" (1962) that raised public awareness. Still it took legislation in the 60s and 70s to get a significant response from society. Finally child abuse is being addressed by legislation, mandated reporting, child protective services and intervention.

While most agencies have long recognized the damage of sexual trauma and included treatment in their programs, some agencies have been slow to face this issue. Reporting of disclosures and formal treatment planning in institutional settings have developed in parallel with the general public. Outside regulators of residential settings helped move agencies toward awareness and response. Compliance around reporting, the first level of response, is fairly well established. But moving beyond compliance to affirmative training to help the abused child in placement is still emerging. This article is an effort to move in this direction by suggesting a training model and by identifying some of the important staff issues in dealing with sexual abuse.

The Two-Headed Conundrum

The gathering of children and young adults together in residential settings presents a conundrum. We face the simultaneous and seemingly conflictual demands of preventing abuse and of healing abuse, of promoting normal sexual development while suppressing abusive, statutory illegal and societal frowned upon sexuality in this population. We must police and protect children from staff to child and from child to child abuse. We must protect residents from the occasional infiltration of staff by a fixated offender (Haddock & McQueen, 1983). But more common is staff inflicted abuse arising from poor conditions of work including job stress, low pay, difficult work conditions, inadequate agency models or protocols and burn out (Atten & Milner, 1987; DiLeonardi & Kelly, 1989; Gillespie & Cohen (1984). Gil (1982) adds an additional form of emotional abuse when the agency's programs involve unfair behavioral management techniques, misuse of diagnosis or medications, denial of home visits, etc.

Yet, beyond creating an abuse free milieu, staff must also be prepared to heal the victims who come into placement. Now staff must encourage disclosure, be ready with therapeutic interventions and support working with the intense feelings. Often the same child presents with both challenges. At least ninety percent of our juvenile sex offenders have been victimized. And if this is not enough, staff must be ready to deal with the seductive, manipulative or vulnerable victim behaviors. How do we train staff to deal effectively with all these aspects?

REDEFINING "STAFF"

"Residential staff" provincially means child care workers and clinical staff. I am applying the word to everyone who comes on grounds for more than a visit or an errand. Like fire safety and payroll procedures, there is some need to know about sex abuse that reaches every individual who spends time in the agency, from the Board to maintenance.

Two of the Board's functions are interfacing with the community and seeing that the Agency staff have the resources to do their work. An uninformed Board cannot explain and advocate to the community nor appreciate what is needed. Board members remain naive and impotent if administration is reluctant to train them about abuse which affects most of the Agency's population and will, with regrettable frequency, hit the local press. Board members should understand what sex abuse is all about and the Agency's written protocols for handling incidents.

Administrators, such as executives and program directors, when dealing with sexual abuse, find that responding to State mandates, critical incidents, press hoopla, staff failures and staff demands to be a form of abuse itself. Yet, they must appreciate that staff supervision, professionalism in child care, organizational issues and staff recruitment are among the most important variables in preventing institutional abuse (Reyome, 1990). Administration is the ship's bridge crew–and a ship can run a true course only if the bridge crew is competent. Achieving administrative competency in understanding, programming and supporting work around sex abuse is a far cry from the orphanage days of steering the agency towards "clean rooms and quiet kids," with efforts to support the myth that abuse does not exist in our Agency.

Among the most important staff segment in preventing and healing abuse in residential settings is child care. Child care has the greatest impact on the residents by nature of the time and the relationships shared with them. While Trieschman et al. (1969) did not specify abuse, they did describe the reality that residents are most influenced by the day-by-day milieu. Blatt and Brown (1986) were able to relate reports of abuse in state psychiatric facilities over a three year period to changes in staff routines. Only a fire alarm should keep a child care worker from a training session on sex abuse.

I once spoke with a clinical worker who, assigned to 20 adolescent girls in residence, unabashedly said, "I don't talk about rape and violent things like that. It makes me feel too uncomfortable thinking that those things happen." Grounds for dismissal! Firemen exist to go into burning buildings, not simply to polish trucks and drive through traffic. Likewise, clinical workers who can not deal with these issues should find work in other settings. They share with child care the greatest need to know.

Support staff include a lot of important people. If you were a child in residence you would know how important kitchen, maintenance, transportation and business personnel are as potential support figures and role models. These are the "real" people who do not have a jargon to speak, an agenda to promote, a one-sided relationship or "professional" distance to keep. And residents reach out to these real people in undervalued ways. The basics of both preventing and healing abuse should be in these real peoples' repertoire. We all know how the wrong word from a telephone receptionist can occupy a resident's and staff's entire afternoon! Again, there is a need to know.

But surely the people in the business office do not have to deal with these "sordid" issues! A payroll clerk who never sees residents, nor even staff, but only time cards and computer printouts should be saved from it. The personnel office needs only satisfy the State requirement of checking new applicants against a register of known abusers. With no further contact with residents or staff, it seems these people may not need any abuse training. You might be right. But consider that they just might encounter a resident in the parking lot. And they do interact in the community. And an uninformed employee is a poor public relations risk. They also have some need to know.

If the agency has a school component, its faculty and staff share in the "need to know" and typically wonder how much "counseling" they should do (Krenk, 1984). While the primary focus of a therapeutic educational program is to help residents learn how to use public school again, basic competency for teachers around abuse is essential. This would help them understand why many of the residents behave the way they do, and would facilitate their management of student problems with faculty and with learning. Education staff need the basics of prevention, reporting and understanding. They do not need the "juicy" information on each resident, but do need to know why this child is resisting authority or setting himself up to be in trouble, dynamics which may arise from abuse experiences.

So Everyone Needs a Master's Degree in Sexual Abuse?

Let's not get messianic. While everyone has a role, not all members need the same information, protocols nor support in relation to abuse. The Board's orientation and the child care's continuing training around abuse should be like crude and kerosene–two forms of oil but very different levels of refinement. Below I offer a matrix for differentiating levels of training in relation to staff needs.

FOUR LEVELS OF STAFF PREPAREDNESS

A Matrix for Staff Preparedness

Levels of training for different staff groups are based simply on differentiating staff who are "involved with the agency," in "contact" with residents, who "work" with residents and those who "supervise" other staff. Each level should involve not simply more time, but a deeper level of attitude and skill development along with an additional knowledge base. The following schema condenses my suggestions for consideration.

Four Levels of Staff Training

The first level I call orientation. All staff–that's all staff: volunteers, students, Board, every new person, even laborers who will be in the buildings for a couple of weeks or more–should have an orientation around abuse, and around confidentiality, and how to relate to the residents, much as they are oriented on how to get out of the building quickly, etc. This may be enough for the business office and the Board.

The second level is basic training with its three components; cognitive understanding, attitude development and skills rehearsal. The orientation turns the naive citizen into (1) an informed and prepared "in-house" mandated reporter, (2) a person with an understanding ear and in-house referral source for residents, and (3) an effective liaison person for the general public should the agency's name come up. The difference between orientation and basic training is the difference between turning to others (orientation) and handling it yourself by following well set protocols.

The third level I call advanced training with the hope that it means something other than "refried beans"–or more of the same! Advanced training results in staff who are "practitioners" of abuse prevention and healing. At this level, they can be trusted to appreciate and respond to incidents quickly and appropriately–whether to keep the residents safe or to help those who have been abused to recover. I feel that any staff who have worked directly with residential children for two years or more should be at this practitioner level!

Then there is supervisor's training, the level reached by staff who have the knowledge, attitude and skills to train new staff, supervise them, and follow them to competent practice. Gillespie and Cohen (1984) report that a poor worker-supervisor relationship leads to worker dissatisfaction and burn out–a major factor in staff abusing residents. DiLeonardi and Kelly (1989) also found inadequate supervision to be a major contributor to staff abuse of residents. Supervising staff are also the people who give the training, who present at conferences and who give guidance during crisis incidents. Any staff over four years, whether they are line supervisors, department directors, or "just" senior line workers should be trained at this level.

STAFF NEEDS AND TRAINING LEVELS

Bare bones curriculum. It is not within the purview of this paper to articulate a full curriculum for training in abuse for residential settings. Krenk (1984) suggested a needs assessment with a training consultant to start with. But, the didactic curriculum is not infinite and is well reviewed in the literature. I would prefer to emphasize some facets of staff needs based on my experience as a staff psychologist and as a consultant to agencies. While consultants are one step removed, the role often allows a level of honest feedback and of observation not available within the staff milieu.

Some may wonder if heightened staff training in abuse may lead to heightened sexual acting out among the residents. Krenk (1984) reported that this phenomenon did not occur after their extensive staff training program.

Level 1–Orientation

Orientation transforms the naive layman into an informed person, one prepared on the level of a mandated reporter. The first goal of orientation is to prepare everyone in the agency to know what to do if they observe a suspicious situation and who, in the agency, they are to report to. They differentiate between restraint and abuse and understand the dynamics of abuse. And they know who to talk to from among the staff.

The second goal of orientation is to prepare everyone involved with the Agency to know how to relate to the community if sexual abuse comes up in conversation. I would hope that all the agency's family of people could quell the public's all too frequent image of residential settings as "hot beds" of sexual exploitation and deviancy. There exists among many a prurient perception of residences for youngsters that is based on B-grade movies like "Girls in Cages" or "Boys on Boys Behind Bars." Let us make sure our agency representatives are beyond this! Far beyond this! Let us make sure that everyone associated with the agency can dispel this form of community abuse of our residents.

Figure 1 outlines the basic level of staff preparedness for everyone who spends time on the Agency's grounds. Moving people from naive ignorance and/or denial to a reasonable state of readiness to help a child and assure prevention, in three hours, is a challenge. The cognitive objectives (see Figure 1) are not the challenge. Much of the material in the University of the State of New York's (1990) mandated reporter training, the "Identification and Reporting of Child Abuse and Neglect" is helpful.

During the orientation, many participants experience a loss of innocence. They are faced with previously unthinkable situations of sexual abuse. Strong reactions may arise, ranging from abhorrence to prurient curiosity and arousal. While these responses are normal, they are not always acceptable to the participants and some time for reflection and discussion may be needed, to help them assimilate the realities of child abuse. One of the most common reactions I have experienced in orientation sessions is disbelief, which serves to temper participant's reactions. It is important not to argue against

Figure 1.

	ORIENTATION
Who attends.	All staff associated with the agency: Board, volunteers, trainees, contractors spending over two weeks in agency, and all new staff.
The goal.	Knowledge and attitudes to act as a mandated reporter within the Agency and to represent the agency appropriately in the community.
How often.	One time.
How long.	Three hours.
When.	Before employment, or as soon as possible.
Format.	Presentation which invites attendees reflection and questions.
Topics include:	1. Awareness of the reality of child abuse in society and in residential placement.
	2. Understanding the abuse program and protocols of the agency.
	3. Awareness of appropriate attitudes needed to protect the residents and the agency.
	4. Awareness of the appropriate attitudes needed to heal those who are victims.
	5. Knowledge of who in the agency to report suspicious behavior or child disclosures to.
	6. Knowledge of what messages to communicate in the community if abuse and the agency's name comes up.

the disbelief. Orientation gently introduces the realities while giving space for the participants to absorb these realities, the attitudes needed to respond to suspicious situations and the permission to use the resources of those more experienced staff who can accept questions and handle in-house reports.

In leading the orientation, I offer a caveat. Orientation is not a soul searching "happening" of self-disclosure featuring personal victimization histories. It should not be run by a zealous clinician demanding catharsis nor a messianic crusader who sees abuse all around. The program simply allows a format in which participants can reflect on the material offered and their personal reactions to it–with a presentation of the attitudes and skills needed to support, protect and heal at this beginner's level.

Level 2–Basic Training

The military gives all recruits "basic training"–so that no matter what type of military career or how high they may go up the chain of command–they know how to fire a rifle, how to clean it, eat in the field and sleep on the ground, in case the need ever arises. Every staff in contact with residents should have enough basic training to follow protocols if faced with incidents like our twenty year old child care worker mentioned in the opening paragraph. Figure 2 offers a paradigm for basic training in residential abuse response.

The basic training curriculum should emphasize the step by step protocols of what to do, who to contact, how to react and how to debrief in abuse incidents. Peter and Daly (1988) emphasize the importance of an agency's "model." "In a safe environment staff need to know what to do as well as what not to do" (Ibid., p. 59).

In consulting with residential staffs, it appears to me that much training focuses on the cognitive information needed, but falls short on the attitude development and skills rehearsal required. Most everyone is uneasy with sexual topics and young staff have many questions about acceptable sexual behavior among residents. Ment and Farragher (1991), in "Romance and Residential Treatment," describe some guidelines around these questions. Before the training at the Christie School, "staff members either tended to underreact, deny or avoid dealing with children's past sexual molestation, or

Figure 2.

```
                        BASIC TRAINING
Who attends.    All staff in contact with residents, including
                business, maintenance, etc. and professionals.
The goal.       The knowledge and attitudes needed to follow
                the agency's protocols around sexual abuse.
How often.      One time.
How long.       A series of three sessions, each three hours.
When.           During first months of employment.
Format.         Brief presentations with structured
                experiential exercises and maximum discussion.
Topics include: Basic knowledge and attitudes to successfully:
                1. Intervene to protect by stopping observed
                   abuse.
                2. To report quickly to appropriate
                   supervisor.
                3. To respond appropriately if a child
                   discloses abuse.
                4. To manage abusive or seductive behaviors.
                5. To separate personal reactions from
                   residents' needs.
                6. To understand the causes, damage to child
                   and legal aspects of abuse.
                7. To follow agency protocols and supervisory
                   directions in abuse situations.
```

they tended to overreact, overexplore or make extreme judgments about how children or parents must feel or behave" resulting in "rescuing" behaviors (Krenk, 1984, p. 172). One effect of training was a "desensitization" allowing staff to put things in perspective.

When staff become personally involved in situations of sexual abuse, either by intervening with victims or having to confront offending residents, they often experience strong reactions within themselves. Some of these reactions are post traumatic phenomena and require debriefing. In support groups and with individuals, we find upsetting dreams, suspiciousness upon seeing single men with a young child in a shopping mall, uneasiness with one's own children or spouse and some obsessional preoccupations. These reactions last about a month and gradually pass. As they occur, supportive messages can help staff greatly. Staff preparedness should anticipate these reactions during basic training.

And so "basic training" must include some safe structured exercises, like the values clarification exercises, and development of attitudes and skills which prepare staff to quickly follow the agency's protocols. Role-play of simulated situations can be used, including stopping two residents engaged sexually, rehearsing the protocol for reporting within the agency, listening and being supportive during a spontaneous disclosure, asking questions and gathering information when first hearing from a staff (or resident) of a suspected incident, rehearsing how to talk to the public when asked questions about "sex in the agency" and to whom to refer the questioner.

Goals at this level are achieved (Krenk, 1984) when staff demonstrate the ability to identify victim symptomatology and treatment needs, to differentiate between normal and abuse related sexual behavior among residents, and to value individual and group therapy specifically designed to remedy the trauma of sexual abuse.

Level 3–Advanced Training

Experienced child care and clinical staffs should be the "practitioners" of abuse work. Their knowledge, attitudes and skills should ensure abuse free management of residents and the ability to assist in the healing of the victims.

Some may question whether child care workers should be trained to become involved in the sensitive work of this type. This concern was addressed, if not put to rest, almost a quarter of a century ago in "The Other 23 Hours" (Trieschman, Whittaker, & Brendtro, 1969). Problems like abuse do not wait for the therapeutic hour of the clinician. Child care must respond when and where the action is. A therapeutic milieu not prepared to prevent and heal abuse may be abusive itself (Gil, 1982). Child care and clinical staff have differential roles as practitioners in the treatment of child sexual abuse. The former provide the safe and healing milieu while the latter focus on the individual and group work involved in the process.

Figure 3 delineates how residential staff can move from inductee status to practitioners of abuse prevention and healing. All staff working with residents need to know (1) how to ensure a therapeutic milieu, (2) how to support cathartic disclosure (Collins & Gabor, 1988), and (3) how to respond to symptoms of Post Traumatic

Stress Disorder as it applies to the cottage program (Oles, 1991). Zahn (1991) describes a multimodal therapeutic program for survivors of abuse.

To complement cognitive learning, structured exercises help prepare the staff's skills. Rehearsals of situations simulating an interview with two girls found in bed together, steps to take coming upon two boys molesting a third, enacting a response to a colleague seen caressing a resident, gathering information from residents and staff about alleged incidents–and much discussion of the staff's reactions to these scenarios typify the kind of attitude and skill rehearsal training needed.

Figure 3.

```
                        ADVANCED TRAINING
Who attends.    Staff working directly with residence in child
                care and clinical areas.
The goal.       The knowledge, attitudes and skills needed to
                work as a "practitioner" around abuse within
                a team format.
How often.      Ongoing.  Four to Six sessions a year and
                ongoing with treatment plans and programs.
How long.       Varies.
When.           Following the basic training activities.
Format.         Presentations, seminars, personalized
                discussion, and structured exercises
                periodically during the year and the
                consultation and support of ongoing
                supervision.
Topics include: Ongoing staff development leading to:
                1. Demonstrate an advanced knowledge base
                   around abuse.
                2. Reliability to handle preventative
                   incidents..
                3. Reliability to handle in-house response
                   protocols and reporting requirements.
                4. Reliability to use supervision for personal
                   support and to validate interventions.
                5. Reliability to participate in the treatment
                   plan of victims to aid their healing.
                6. Reliability to respond to incidents
                   independently and follow up by reporting to
                   treatment team.
```

On the Job Training

While a solid curriculum should be followed over time, Daly (1985) supports my position that only 20% of learning is in the classroom and 80% is on the job. The training described above is planned, scheduled and delivered to staff–and hopefully verified through the personnel records–over the first three months. But firemen and airplane pilots do not learn their crafts at annual courses. Like these professionals, residential staff learn on the job. Preparing staff to prevent and heal abuse must be ongoing in the regular team treatment planning and review meetings.

The emotional needs of staff at this level changes in my experience. The reactions typical of post trauma are rarer and occur only if increasingly horrendous situations of abuse are disclosed. Allegations among staff may once again trigger the trauma stress patterns, but a tolerance develops among staff. Indeed, some staff become blasé, even cynical of abuse situations. This is a real danger in terms of the need of the milieu to be protective. Some staff become messianic and impose their expectations of how residents must be reacting and may even further victimize the resident while believing they are helping. As at each level of training, time for reflection, permission for discussion and structured sharing enhance the possibility of staff maintaining a balanced response.

Level 4–Supervisory Training

Where does an agency get the expertise to develop an ideal staff development program? Are special grants or donations needed to engage consultants? Not really–the knowledge and experience base is sitting right in our agencies! An outside consultant might be helpful the first time around (Krenk, 1984), but only to help identify and organize the materials, curriculum, protocols and support systems. After that, a good administrator–someone organized with clear thinking and good planning ability–can come from in-house staff. And that is where the supervisory and administrative staff of the agency can shine. Figure 4 outlines the preparedness of management.

Figure 4.

SUPERVISORY TRAINING	
Who attends.	All supervisory staff and administrators of direct resident's services.
The goal.	The knowledge, attitudes and skills needed to train, supervise and support other staff around abuse.
How often.	Ongoing - four to six activities a year and ongoing with treatment planning and programs.
How long.	Varies. An initial three hour session on supervising around sexual issues and sexual abuse, followed with on the job supervision.
When.	Before promotion as a supervisor or as soon as possible; then ongoing.
Format.	Presentations, seminars, personalized discussions, and structured exercises.
Topics include:	1. Competence to carry out the agency's abuse program.
	2. Competence to train other staff in abuse response.
	3. Competence to contribute to updating the agency's abuse protocols.
	4. Competence to train non-agency professionals in abuse.

An Enigma of Supervision

Endemic in many organizations is the promotion of excellent staff to positions of supervision or management without adequate preparation and training. Excelling line staff are moved up the ladder and then flounder in the absence of formal training and support around the unfamiliar role of managing other people. Developing a strong program in abuse prevention and healing requires a well trained and supportive supervisory staff.

By the time of their promotion, supervisory and department administrators should be among the "professionals" in the field of sexual abuse. Now they must be trained to lead others in this work. They will join the cadre of experts and teachers of other human services workers. The need for this cadre is emphasized by Daly (1985) who, along with others, suggests that motivated and well supported staff rarely abuse children while burned out staff do abuse children (Ibid., p. 37). With a coach or monitor which staff can use (which speaks to the quality of supervision) they develop the art and craft of healing and insure a milieu of safety.

A major challenge for supervisor preparedness occurs when allegations are leveled at one of their line workers. Helping staff remain appropriate while the grapevine buzzes and the investigation and the final outcome are processed is very difficult. The challenge here is great, the work important but the development of these skills extremely rewarding to the supervisory staff.

The emotional needs of staff now turn from their response to sex abuse to their feelings and attitudes about leading other staff in areas of the residents' sexual development as well as around abuse. It is often a difficult shift for new supervisors to see themselves working with staff–not with residents! The hardest part usually is confronting negative attitudes, mistakes and inadequacies of line staff. Feeling emotionally strong with staff becomes the challenge.

Experiential learning is needed and can rely on role play and "post mortems" of simulated and actual case scenarios. Practicing, with feedback, on interviewing a staff member who has experienced an allegation, supervising a debriefing session for a resident raped during off campus, practicing phone conversations with distraught parents, and enacting communicating with an external investigator, all typify the kinds of skill-development techniques recommended at this level. Participants should do some "practice teaching" to each other with feedback, watch and critique a taped or simulated internal investigation, and rehearse "coaching" a new staff with peer review. The product is a supervisor who can teach, coach, support and correct line staff as they learn to respond to abuse.

In conclusion let me raise two questions. How can we prevent abuse in our residential settings and where should we go for the expertise to heal our residents? Staff preparedness is the answer to both. As Bloom, Denton and Caflish (1991) elaborate, staff preparedness involves protection for the child, support for the staff and maintaining the agency's needs. A prepared agency protects and heals.

And where is the expertise? Ten years ago, one was limited to the pioneers, those who first worked and wrote about their work in sex abuse. Now that abuse response is not new, the expertise is no longer sparse. Since residential staff deals with a disproportionate number of victims and emerging abusers, it seems logical to look for the expertise here "in the field of residential care!" It seems appropriate that residential centers should join specialized abuse treatment centers as resources for professionals and the community at large.

The supervisory staff of residential centers should be among the leaders, trainers and program designers. The agencies already have the population, the need, the staff, the training programs and the experience. We can take the lead. We can move from "beleaguered agencies" reacting to internal and external pressures around child abuse to a position of professional leadership and preparedness.

REFERENCES

Atten, D.W. & Milner, J.S. (1987). Child abuse potential and work satisfaction in day care employees. *Child Abuse and Neglect, 11,* 117-123.

Blatt, E. & Brown, S. (1986). Environmental influences on incidents of alleged child abuse and neglect in New York State psychiatric facilities: Toward an etiology of institutional child maltreatment. *Child Abuse and Neglect, 10,* 171-180.

Bloom, R.; Denton, I.R. & Caflish, C. (1991). Institutional sexual abuse: A crisis in trust. In *Contributions to Residential Treatment 1991,* American Association of Children's Residential Centers: Washington, D.C., 33-47.

Collins, D. & Gabor, P. (1988). Helping children with cathartic disclosure of trauma. *Journal of Child Care, 3,* 25-38. *Challenging the limits of care,* Trieschman Center: Needham, MA.

Daly, D.L. & Peter, V.J. (1988). Promoting safe environments in residential care. In Small, R.W. & Alwon, F.J. (Eds.), *Challenging the limits of care.* The Albert E. Trieschman Center: Needham, MA.

DiLeonardi, J. & Kelly, E. (1989). Preventing and managing child abuse in group care: Report and recommendations of a survey in practice. In Balcerzak, E.A. (Ed.), *Group care of children: Transitions toward the year 2000.* Washington, D.C.: Child Welfare League of America, Inc.

Gil, E. (1982). Institutional abuse of children in out-of-home care. *Child and Youth Care Review, 4,* 7-13.

Gillespie, D.F. & Cohen, S.E. (1984). Causes of worker burnout. *Children and Youth Services Review, 6,* 115-124.

Haddock, H.D. & McQueen, W.M. (1983). Assessing employee potentials for abuse. *Journal of Clinical Psychology, 39,* 1021-1029.

Kempe, C.H.; Silverman, F.N. & Steele, B.F. (1962). The battered child syndrome. *Journal of the American Medical Association, 181,* 17-24.

Krenk, C.J. (1984). Training residence staff for child abuse treatment. *Child Welfare League of America, 68,* 167-173.

Ment, N.W. (1991). Romance and residential treatment. In *Contributions to Residential Treatment.* American Association of Children's Residential Centers, Washington, D.C.

Oles, T.P. (1991). Complementing the therapist: Child care work with sexually abused youth. *Journal of Child and Youth Care, 5,* 43-50.

Peter, V.J. & Daly, D.L. (1988). Promoting safe environments in residential care. In R.W. Small & F.J. Alwon (Eds.).

Powers, J.L.; Mooney, A. & Nunno, M. (1990). Institutional abuse: A review of the literature. *Journal of Child and Youth Care, 4,* 81-94.

Reyome, N.D. (1990). Executive directors' perceptions of the prevention of child abuse and maltreatment in residential facilities. *Journal of Child and Youth Care, 4,* 45-60.

Rindfleisch, N. & Rabb, J. (1984). How much of a problem is resident maltreatment in child welfare institutions? *Child Abuse and Neglect, 8,* 33-40.

Trieschman, A.E.; Whittaker, J.K. & Brendtro, L.K. (1969). *The other 23 hours.* Aldine: Chicago.

University of the State of New York (1990). The identification and reporting of child abuse and maltreatment. New York State Education Department, Albany, New York.

Zahn, B.S. (1991). The survivors project: A new multimodal therapy program for adolescents who have survived child sexual abuse. In *Contributions to Residential Treatment 1991,* American Association of Children's Residential Centers: Washington, D.C., 105-123.

Experiences with Alleged Sexual Abuse in Residential Program: I. Case Vignettes

Wander de C. Braga, MD

SUMMARY. The systematic study of sexual abuse in residential and other institutional settings is a relatively new area of research interest. The author stresses the importance of naturalistic studies, which are sorely lacking in the extant literature. He presents four case vignettes and briefly discusses each of them. The purpose is to illustrate the wide variety of complex circumstances that are categorized as alleged sexual abuse, and to comment on the learned lessons as these cases were managed clinically and administratively. The importance of accumulating and disseminating knowledge derived from such an approach is emphasized.

Allegations of sexual abuse occur all too frequently in residential programs. Their management is difficult because they elicit a great

Dr. Braga wishes to express his gratitude to his secretary, Mrs. Florence Yanko, for her tireless efforts in typing and helping organize this material.

He may be contacted at 60 Academy Road, Albany, NY 12208. Views and opinions expressed in this paper are the author's own and in no way should they be construed as representing philosophy, policies or procedures of the agencies with which he is associated.

deal of anxiety, fear, guilt, and feelings of vulnerability in the entire treatment and administrative systems. These feelings are com- pounded by concerns about accountability and liability which have escalated, given recent mandated reporting and investigatory stat- utes. This article intends to raise questions, point out learned les- sons and propose ideas that may be fruitful to others confronted with similar problems.

Sexual abuse within institutions is a relatively new field of study. Consequently, naturalistic studies that emphasize the clear-minded observation of life without idealization, pre-conceived notions, or avoidance of the ugly are important. Findings and conclusions of such studies should be shared with other practitioners, families, certi- fying, funding and monitoring bodies, as well as those creating pub- lic policy. Controlled studies that employ a discreet scientific meth- odology (i.e., operational definitions, measurements, tables and statistics) are undeniably most important, but they are often most useful when they complement, rather than supplant, naturalistic observation. This is especially so in a field where knowledge is incipient.

Herein, the author capitalizes on a few cases that came to his attention while working as a psychiatric consultant to various thera- peutic settings in the years 1984-1991. However, while writing this article, he became keenly aware of two important features. Firstly, abusive circumstances are very heterogeneous, defying classifica- tion. Secondly, the interest for an open, dispassionate and scientifi- cally-oriented approach to this topic conflicts with tangible and intangible realities. These matters are heavily value-laden and, in addition, powerful liability concerns do exist in reality. Personnel matters, confidentiality issues, staff's rights, legal and statutory pro- visions, all combine to create intractable situations when one wishes to publish on this topic. This is an undeniable "social reality." These considerations are probably reflected in the dearth of literature on this subject, which prompted Kennedy's (1991) assertion:

> . . . Surely this lack of material on such an important subject reflects the great hesitation of psychiatric institutions to reveal such matters to the public . . . . (p. 24)

Due to the importance of such studies, ways to minimize against the problems cited need to be considered. Cooperative multi-center studies that pool cases from several writers might be one such method. In this study the author chose to manage this problem by presenting case vignettes. These have been disguised sufficiently to protect confidentiality, but effort was made to maintain content areas unaltered. Some of these vignettes are detailed and will be followed immediately by comments; others are briefer.

CASE 1

Events in this case occurred prior to the implementation of the New York Child Abuse Prevention Act of 1985.

Celia, an attractive 16-year old Caucasian girl, was accepted for treatment in a residential program after her adjudication as a juvenile delinquent by a Family Court. She had been chronically truant from school, lied, smoked marijuana and was disruptive in classes. Her J.D. adjudication occurred as a result of her setting fire and totally destroying a community center in her town. A diagnosis of Conduct Disorder was made at admission.

During intake staff was informed that Celia had alleged sexual abuse against her mother's boyfriend, and authorities in her community were investigating it. The boyfriend was said to drink to excess and to rely heavily on corporal punishment to discipline the children. The girl's mother appeared loving and devoted to her children but she was rather conflicted in her loyalties between children and boyfriend. She had faced financial difficulties earlier in life and was determined not to jeopardize her current stability, largely provided by the boyfriend. She shared with staff, however, that she found her relationship to him less than satisfactory; Celia, on the other hand, consistently coaxed her mother to leave the boyfriend.

In treatment, Celia maintained her allegation of sexual abuse by her mother's boyfriend, his corporal punishment of her as well as her siblings, and her fears that "he will kill me if I go back home." While mother participated in family therapy, the boyfriend avoided therapeutic contacts. The girl disclosed that this man had never penetrated her sexually, but he had undressed in front of her and fondled her in bed. Mother rationalized this behavior as his efforts to teach the girl "the facts of life." Celia further revealed that an older brother had also attempted to molest her, but details never were known.

Celia came across to staff as an assertive, surly, intelligent but oppositional and defiant client. She was rather uncomfortable with heterosexual relationships. While having many boys as friends, she never had a boyfriend while in the program, despite many suitors. Also, there was never any indication of sexual acting-out on her part.

Some six or seven months into her treatment, consideration as to the implementation of her discharge plan began dominating her therapeutic management. The girl refused to return to her home as long as the boyfriend was there; she continued imploring her mother to leave him. The mother then came up with the idea of sending Celia out of town to live with her maternal grandmother. This woman, who lived several thousand miles away, had taken care of Celia as a little child, and there was a positive bond between them. Of course, the treatment team felt quite uncomfortable with this "solution." Yet, Celia preferred the idea of leaving town as opposed to returning home. Contact was established with grandmother who, after many calls and letters, decided that she could not possibly take care of a teenager. Celia felt doubly abandoned.

It was in the context of this intense personal dilemma that Celia, now nearing the end of her seventh month of treatment, complained to a child care worker that a young male worker in the night shift had attempted to sexually molest her. Her story was that this child care worker entered her room while she was asleep and fondled her breasts, which woke her up. She then saw him "fiddling" with her bed sheets as though pretending that he was covering her. She proceeded yelling at him to leave her room, which he did.

The allegation came to the attention of a program director who quickly consulted with a child psychiatrist who worked with that residential unit. It was the latter's opinion that in all likelihood Celia had experienced a type of sleep-related phenomenon: suddenly wakened by the child care worker in her room, she construed the experience to conform with expectations of abuse which she was likely to have experienced earlier at home. It was known that the boyfriend had been in charge of the children mostly at night when the mother was at work, information which strengthened the dynamic hypothesis mentioned above. At this point in the unfolding sequence of events, the inclination of staff was to disbelieve the girl's accusation. Nevertheless, a report to the "Hot Line" was made and an agency social worker was assigned to investigate the allegation. She repeated her story with consistency and the social worker was left with the conviction that she was telling the truth. A decision was made to suspend the child care worker with pay while more data was gathered (an important consideration since the man worked alone during the night shift). Further information was obtained which indicated that several other child caring institutions in the area had expressed concern about this man because of similar allegations, none substantiated, however. His application form and resume filed with the agency when originally interviewed for his job were scrutinized. This revealed that there was no mention of previous child care institutional experiences but the letters of reference obtained were rather positive. In addition, his reference check for prior history of child abuse, a legally mandated procedure, had come back as a negative one. When a call to the local police was made, it was learned that not only had the accused worker given the agency a pseudonym when hired, but he was wanted by the military authorities for desertion.

While this data was accumulating, interviews with the accused worker revealed contradictory information which ultimately failed to explain his presence in the girl's room. He was arrested soon thereafter by the local police for an unrelated felony, which preempted further prosecution on grounds of sexual abuse.

Of course, as this sequence unfolded, a change of view as to the veracity of Celia's allegations occurred. She was told by staff (even before the worker's desertion charges were known) that she was believed in her allegation. This posture had a very positive effect in her subsequent treatment, particularly in her attitude towards staff and program in general. It was very important for her to be validated, especially since her allegation against mother's boyfriend had been deemed "unfounded" by county authorities charged with its investigation.

This girl was discharged to the care of her mother after eighteen months of treatment. She desperately wished to leave treatment; other discharge options more suitable than a return to home were not found. Follow-up one and two months post-discharge indicated she was adjusting well. Six months later it was learned that mother and boyfriend were planning to separate, as the quasi-conjugal situation continued to deteriorate. It was not known if the presence of Celia in the household contributed to that development.

Comments

1. In residential treatment, allegations of sexual abuse are likely to occur in the context of complex personal, clinical, staff-related and familial variables. Disentangling these variables to ascertain what truly happened is frequently very difficult, but every effort should be made in this direction. Incidents are merely the tip of an iceberg , and dealing with them as disembodied facts leads at best to a partial view of reality and at worst to a very false perspective.

2. Dynamic hypothesis in isolation do not constitute good grounds for conclusions as to the truth or falsehood of allegations. The inner psychological reality and the external reality may sometimes coexist in apparent contradiction (it is jocularly said that even paranoid patients may have real enemies). Systematic fact-finding is of the essence in these situations, which involves the usage of detective-like methods to obtain evidence which are different from the usual clinical approach (Hoorwitz, 1992). However, corroborating facts are frequently hard to come by in sexual allegations. Clinicians must search for congruity between verifiable facts, dynamic thinking and careful interviewing, as pointed out by Heiman (1992).

3. After the occurrence of this incident, many states established more stringent statutes mandating employee pre-hiring screening for record of physical/sexual abuse (i.e., finger-printing and other methods). It is likely that child care agencies have been helped by these laws. Yet, they cannot be entirely trusted as we learned in this case. Exploitative individuals do exist who may selectively seek jobs in child care agencies, perhaps moving from agency to agency to avoid detection. Balancing child protection with civil rights of applicants is a concern likely to take center stage in the future. The

effectiveness of employee screening methods, in itself a controversial matter, will need to wait for greater experience and empirical research for future clarification. In this case, finger-printing might have alerted us for his AWOL status as well as his pseudonym.

4. It appears therapeutic for clients to know that they are believed and validated when their allegations against staff are substantiated. Validation is a complex issue because many situations are not clear cut. Validation can become a tool to advance particular ideologies rather than a clinical intervention. Using an analogy, in clinical laboratory practice test results are classified into four types: positive, negative, false positive and false negative. Investigations of abuse may be conceived as a test, result of which may fall in one of the above-mentioned categories. Of course, validation is legitimate only for the positive type of result. One should recognize, however, that current "zeitgeist" in many clinical settings encourages validation for all four types, apparently in the naive belief that the victim alleging abuse is telling the truth in all instances. Ample literature on false allegations does exist and it should be consulted for details: Benedek, E.P. and Schetky, D.H. (1987a, 1987b); deYoung, M. (1986); Everson, M.O. and Boat, B.W. (1989); Klajner-Diamond et al. (1987); Mantell, D.M. (1988); Wehrspann, W.H. et al. (1987); Gardner, R.A. (1992).

5. A therapeutic impasse is created when allegations occurring outside the program are deemed "unfounded," but staff firmly believes the culpability of the alleged perpetrator (in this case the boyfriend). It may be best for therapists to feel comfortable in saying to such patients: "we do not know what truly happened but we wish to respect your convictions."

6. Clinicians and personnel managers need to collaboratively develop profiles of both the client vulnerable to exploitation and the staff member vulnerable to becoming exploitative. Collins (1989) discusses these points in an article describing sexual abuse in an adult psychiatric setting.

CASE 2

This case occurred after full implementation of the Child Abuse Prevention Act in New York State of 1985. This Act formalized reporting, monitoring, and investigatory procedures, and gave to a body separate from the funding and licensing agency the responsibility to carry out such functions.

Involved in the case were two boys, Carlos, 14.8 years and Tim, 12.9 years who received treatment in two different cottages of a residential program. They left the program during school hours and were found attempting to engage in anal intercourse. Carlos left at 1:55 p.m. after a relatively "good morning," despite his going in and out of the classroom as if play-acting an eventual AWOL. Tim, on the other hand, had been extremely agitated from the moment he arrived in school, requiring two separate doses of "PRN" (as needed) medications ordered that morning by his psychiatrist. His therapist was interviewing him when he stormed out of the school building. The boys met each other on grounds and jointly left the property, with two supervising child care workers immediately following them. They were found in a neighboring sports facility under a tarpaulin covering a high-jump pit. As the supervisors approached the area they heard Tim saying "it hurts." Pulling the tarpaulin back they saw that Carlos' pants were down; he said something about having needed to urinate, but immediately ran away. Tim, who was buttoning his own pants, was held by the staff and immediately became agitated and violent, needing to be restrained. He was brought back to school where he finally settled down. He returned to his residential cottage at the end of the school day, while Carlos returned on his own.

Carlos had a chronic history of emotional disturbance and had received treatment in various settings prior to this admission. Clinically he showed loose thinking, confabulatory ideas, extremes of violent behavior and fire-setting tendencies. His DSM-III-R diagnosis was Atypical Psychosis (Axis I) and Borderline Intellectual Functioning (Axis II). He received regularly 250 mg of Mellaril as part of his comprehensive treatment. It is important to note that four months prior to this incident he had visited with his natural father, whom he had not seen in many years. Since admission to this program he was not known as a boy prone to sexual acting out. However, history indicated that when he was eight years old he was found by his mother in a situation of obvious sexual involvement with a 6.5 year-old boy from his neighborhood. This came to the attention of the younger boy's family who reported the incident to the police. During police investigation, Carlos disclosed that he himself had been sexually molested by his natural father. The police demanded that Carlos and his father submit to polygraph tests; his father "passed" but Carlos "failed" and therefore the case against father was dropped. The boy's mother, however, believed that something had happened between her son and ex-husband for she indicated that it was around that time that her son presented the severest acting out, including fire-setting and an attempt to derail a train (!). In any event, there was no clinical follow-up nor legal consequences regarding Carlos' allegation against his father; his involvement with the younger neighbor boy also resulted in no specific actions.

Tim had been admitted to the residential program approximately one year before this incident. He carried the diagnosis of Overanxious Disorder (Axis I) plus Borderline Intellectual Functioning (Axis II). His course of treatment had been full of turmoil, with Tim going AWOL from either school or residential cottage on a chronic basis. His history indicated that the psychological deterioration leading to his admission related to the disintegration of his natural father's life. This man had lost his job, his house, his wife (boy's step-mother) and the custody of Tim's older brother. He had been unavailable emotionally to Tim, only occasionally visiting and contacting him. Tim's natural mother had abandoned the family years earlier. The boy's psychiatrist formulated a dynamic diagnosis as follows: ". . . Tim has been supporting an escalating state of panic and reactive depression in consequence of the intolerable suspense and interminable isolation from the frail and ephemeral source of emotional support (father) . . . " Complicating matters, one of Tim's brothers died after being struck by a car and the family felt that somehow Tim was to blame. Prior to this incident with Carlos, Tim was not known to have been involved in sexual acting out nor did he have a history of sexual abuse.

Soon after the boys were found, the agency child psychiatrist was notified and asked whether or not the boys should be referred to a local hospital for the so-called "rape kit," an examination designed to yield clinical and legal evidence. Reluctantly, the psychiatrist made the referral, reasoning that this would be important for forensic purposes, even when he questioned the wisdom of exposing these psychiatrically ill children to yet another potentially traumatic experience.

An internal investigation was set up but before it started, a significant number of people and agencies needed to be notified: Child Abuse Hot Line, external investigators, police, State Office of Mental Health, Mental Health Legal Services (which represented Carlos only), guardians, parents, internal supervisory structure of the agency, hospital officials performing examinations on the boys and last, but not least, the public relations office of the agency. With the assignment of an internal investigator, a thorough review of documents took place, including on-call child care logs, the school out-of-program log, incident report forms, manual of policies and procedures re: critical incidents, administrative meeting notes and clinical records. Interviews of relevant people followed, in this case the classroom teacher, the school principal, the staff who retrieved the boys, their social workers and the boys themselves.

As a result of this effort, the following findings were reached:

  a. the boys evaded alert staff and voluntarily left the program;
  b. Tim had exhibited a prolonged crisis prior to this incident as he had left the program sixteen times in the four previous months;
  c. even before the incident, school officials had taken steps to diminish the frequency of AWOL's occurring there;
  d. Carlos had been preoccupied with family matters (i.e., relationship with his natural father) before leaving the premises with Tim;
  e. sexual acting out within the treatment program had not been a pattern for either of these boys prior to the incident;
  f. Carlos' visitation with his father probably stirred up unresolved feelings related to his alleged sexual abuse by the latter and may now have been acted out in the incident;
  g. staff was not negligent in allowing the boys to leave the premises; child care workers followed the children immediately after they left the premises;
  h. there was no indication that force, coercion, intimidation or bribery had been used by one boy against the other.

Before arriving at these conclusions, a determination had been made to notify the external investigatory body of the status of the investigation. The latter decided to initiate their own process. It is worth mentioning that around that time the entire mental health community in the state had been sensitized by a "sex scandal" uncovered at a public psychiatric center. Thus, the "atmosphere" favored a full investigation.

The investigator wished to interview not only Carlos and Tim, but any other child in their respective units deemed necessary. This created an impasse because Tim belonged to a unit outside the jurisdiction of the investigative body (which did have jurisdiction over Carlos' unit). The rationale for the broadened scope of interviews was to determine if a "pattern" of abusive sexual conduct existed in either unit. Lawyers for the agency were consulted and their advice, surprisingly enough, was not to contest the investigator's intent.

Countless hours were spent reviewing documents and interviewing children and staff. Complaints were voiced by some staff that they felt "grilled" by the interrogatory style of interview and treated as though they themselves had committed a crime. Four months after the date of the incident a report was received, stating that no credible evidence of staff neglect had been encountered, therefore the case was deemed "unfounded." Yet, several recommendations were made. Cited among them was the need for internal investigators to obtain written statements from all those interviewed, a procedure at variance with common clinical practice. Also recommended was a review of the agency's child management practices, with the goal of not allowing children to "roam freely" on grounds. Further recommended was the need to amend childrens' treatment plans so that sexual behavior be targeted as a specific goal. The report ended by stipulating a date for a plan of corrections to be submitted; such plan should indicate how the agency proposed to address the above-mentioned recommendations.

COMMENTS

1. The lack of normative data concerning child and adolescent sexual behavior invites automatic categorization of all sexual con-

tacts as either abusive or else pathological, and thus detrimental to development. Normative data is urgently needed for its absence invites the criminalization of all sexual experiences of youth in treatment facilities.

2. To define by legislative fiat that all minors are non-consenting regarding sexual behavior may help legal and para-legal authorities in investigatory and prosecutory activity, but it will not deter children and adolescents from such experiences. It is a curiosity that youthful sexual contact may trigger an investigation possibly resulting in a finding of staff neglect, but the same usually does not occur as related to episodes of violence, which more commonly threatens safety in the environment of residential programs.

3. Thorough investigations, however important they are in uncovering facts, are rather time consuming for either internal or external investigators. Resource allocation is an important consideration here, especially when no earmarked funds have been allocated to residential programs in support of these activities.

4. Violation of appropriate personal boundaries is the essential problem in matters of sexual abuse. Outside investigators, if possessed by messianic zeal, run the risk of violating appropriate boundaries separating agencies and the external world. The rationale commonly used to justify outside monitoring and investigation ("conflict of interest," i.e., agencies cannot be expected to police themselves) needs to be balanced with due regard for the consequences of the use of excessive power. Demoralization of staff and unwillingness to report may be unwelcome consequences, among others.

5. This case illustrates a gross disproportion between stimulus and response. The stimulus: two severely disturbed boys attempt what seemed consensual anal intercourse. The response: they are severely punished with a trip to an Emergency Room for invasive anal, rectal and penile examinations in addition to endless interviews and interrogations. If they had pre-existing feelings of inner wickedness, these must have been reinforced by this procedural extravaganza. Legitimate health concerns (HIV, other sexually transmitted illnesses) could have been dealt with by careful review of existing medical records or other less invasive procedures.

6. To this author's knowledge, the published literature is entirely

silent regarding follow-up studies of unsubstantiated cases. What happens clinically to innocent people who endured this type of investigation? To what extent do existing remedies for this problem further harm or traumatize those involved, especially young children?

7. Child care agencies receiving recommendations from external bodies that monitor alleged abuse in institutions must be extremely careful not to allow that such recommendations spill over areas that transcend abuse, such as broad issues of philosophy of treatment and rationale for treatment goals. Again, maintenance of appropriate boundaries is of the essence.

CASE 3

An 18 year, 10 month old boy got sexually involved with a young female in the educational staff of a public school who also functioned as a volunteer in the residence where this boy received treatment. She was a teacher-assistant and only a few years older than the boy himself. As the Registry was called it was stated that there was no legal case given the age of the alleged victim.

This young man struggled intensely with conflicts related to autonomy and separation from his mother. The latter was perceived by him as overbearing, intrusive and controlling. Further, he was being transitioned from the residence into an adult setting in the community. This made him extremely anxious, particularly because he was also finishing high school. His dependency conflicts, highly aroused at this time of significant changes, apparently found expression in his intimate involvement with someone he possibly saw as a "benign" authority figure. Similar dynamic features were reported by Kennedy (Ibid.):

> ... Patients often experience discharge from psychiatric hospitals as a powerfully traumatic separation. They may at such times seek out nurturance and reassurance from staff members ... [Such] longings can become easily confused as overtures for sexual attention ... (Staff) may become caught up in these experiences and engage in sexual misconduct with the patient .... (pp 24-25)

Clearly, the teacher-assistant actions were a violation of agency policy and an infringement of professional ethics. This case illustrates the importance for various professional and para-professional organizations (those of physicians, psychologists, social workers, teachers, clergy, lawyers, nurses, child care workers, and mental health technicians) to formulate, disseminate, train, and advocate that their members adhere by a code of ethics which explicitly proscribes sexual behavior in the work sphere. Special attention is needed in connection with para-professionals, who exist in relatively large numbers in residential programs.

Pope (1989) comments on teacher-student sexual involvement:

> . . . if therapist sex is something we have neglected, the teacher-student sex is something we hardly acknowledge. Even our most probing texts tend to be silent on this subject . . . It is a phenomenon which, on the professional level, is not seen, is not heard, and is not discussed . . . . (p 164)

Cases like this are very difficult to be managed because gossip, scapegoating and blame tend to spread like a brush fire throughout the treatment system. Policies and procedures that specify a "need to know" philosophy (which limits the number of people informed about the event) only go so far in containing the spread of information and misinformation through the "grapevine."

CASE 4

A 17 year old girl diagnosed with a psychotic condition complained that a male nurse teaching a class on biology of reproduction had made lewd comments about her anatomy. The complaint surfaced weeks after the alleged incident had occurred. The nurse adamantly denied the accusation. An investigation was initiated but soon became entangled in an undecipherable conglomeration of statements and counter statements which, by installments, ended up involving three other girls in the program. The investigator probably felt as if watching Kurosawa's classic "Rashomon." In this cinematic masterpiece, a story is told from three different perspectives, each utterly believable yet each quite different from the others in significant aspects.

Early as the investigation unfolded, the accused perpetrator threatened to sue the agency. Later he left his employment abruptly and unexpectedly. This case left many doubts in the minds of those involved in its management as to what truly happened. The accuser was a previously sexually abused girl, quite prone to dramatics, who was known to distort reality. Her allegations surfaced in installments, and corroborative evidence from others was at best ambiguous. Whether the nurse-teacher was simply insensitive to the fact that he was dealing with emotionally disturbed girls who might distort comments or actions (even if done in the best of intentions), or whether he was "grooming" the girls to later exploit them, it never became clear.

Clinicians and staff in general will need to cultivate their own tolerance for ambiguity, for cases such as the above are likely to occur with frequency. Specialized training for those teaching sexually abused youth is a must. Issues of transference and counter transference, as pointed out by Ponce (1989), are of crucial importance. Supervisors need to be very attentive to details in the staff-client relationship that indicate the erosion of appropriate boundaries separating professional and recipient of services. Nurses, much like any other discipline working closely with children and adolescents, are vulnerable to becoming targets of allegations; they also may act out abusively towards children and adolescents. The teaching of human sexuality is a rather complicated matter best left to those specially trained in this field, particularly when classes include sexually abused youth.

CONCLUSION

In the public mind, reference to sexual abuse in institutions is likely to evoke stereotyped images of powerful and predatory adult staff viciously taking advantage of defenseless boys and girls. To the extent that the sample illustrated here is representative of actual situations faced by residential programs generally, it follows that the reality is different and much more complex.

The first case here described ("Celia") might indeed have progressed to fit the above-mentioned stereotype. That outcome did not occur, however, because the girl's first allegation triggered an internal investigation which resulted in the validation of her claim against a staff member. The importance of taking seriously such allegations and the need to add to specific clinical approaches a fact-finding methodology are stressed.

The second case ("Carlos" and "Tim") features child-to-child sexual involvement. An internal investigation and its results are described. Mandated reporting triggered an outside investigation and problems that surfaced during its course are described and commented upon.

The third case features adult-to-adult sexual involvement. It belongs more properly in the area of breach of professional (or para-professional) ethics rather than child abuse. It illustrates that designations such as "victim" and "perpetrator" are simplifications of very complex relationship problems. In this case the small age difference between participants was probably an important factor, a feature common in adolescent residential programs.

The fourth case, rather equivocal as to what happened, illustrates the difficulty in ascertaining the truth in many such cases. It also illustrates that nurses, much as other disciplines working closely with residents, are not immune from being implicated in such allegations.

A point is made that thorough investigations, either internal or external, are rather time-consuming and labor-intensive. They impinge powerfully on the issue of resource allocation, an issue most relevant to residential programs since they usually operate on stringent budgets. With Pollyannish hope, several of my colleagues have mentioned the need for a new and special funding stream dubbed "legal per diem," analogous to the existing "medical per diem," to supplement rates currently afforded agencies and to properly support such investigations.

Finally, an important lesson learned is that naturalistic studies such as this are very difficult to be conducted and published with candor. The right to confidentiality of those involved in incidents, the potential for undue influence of legal and regulatory processes, and the fear of those even distantly involved in an incident that public association with it will result in prejudicial treatment or legal vulnerabilities, are all factors which, however frustrating to the student of sexual abuse in institutions, are real, and cannot be ignored with impunity. Yet, searching for the best approximation of the truth is crucial, not only for the sake of knowledge, but because everyday practice is being powerfully affected by public policy whose underlying assumptions need substantiation based on empirical findings.

REFERENCES

Benedek, E.P. & Schetky, D.H. (1987a). Problems in validating allegations of sexual abuse. I. Factors affecting perception and recall of events. *Journal of the American Academy of Child and Adolescent Psychiatry, 26,* 912-915.

Benedek, E.P. & Schetky, D.H. (1987b). Problems in validating allegations of sexual abuse. II. Clinical Evaluation. *Journal of the American Academy of Child and Adolescent Psychiatry, 26,* 916-921.

Collins, D.T. (1989). Sexual involvement between psychiatric hospital staff and their patients. In Gabbard, G.O. (Ed.), *Sexual exploitation in professional relationships.* Washington, D.C.: American Psychiatric Press.

deYoung, M. (1986). A conceptual model for judging the truthfulness of a young child's allegation of sexual abuse. *American Journal of Orthopsychiatry, 56,* 550-559.

Everson, M.O. & Boat, B.W. (1989). False allegations of sexual abuse by children and adolescents. *Journal of the American Academy of Child and Adolescent Psychiatry, 28,* 230-235.

Gardner, R.A. (1992). *True and false accusations of child sex abuse.* Cresskill, NJ: Creative Therapeutics.

Heiman, M.L. (1992). Annotation: Putting the puzzle together: Validating allegations of child sexual abuse. *Journal of Child Psychology and Psychiatry, 33,* 311-329.

Kennedy, L.L. (1991). Staff-patient sexual relationships disrupts entire therapeutic system. *The Psychiatric Times, 8* (3), 24-27.

Klajner-Diamond, H. et al. (1987). Assessing the credibility of young children's allegations of sexual abuse: Clinical issues. *Canadian Journal of Psychiatry, 32,* 610-614.

Mantell, D.M. (1988). Clarifying erroneous child sexual abuse allegations. *American Journal of Orthopsychiatry, 58,* 618-621.

Ponce, D. (1991). Erotic counter-transference issues in a residential treatment center. In *Contributions to Residential Treatment,* Washington, D.C.: AACRC, pp. 21-32.

Pope, K.S. (1989). Teacher-student sexual intimacy. In Gabbard, G.O. (Ed.), *Sexual exploitation in professional relationships.* Washington, D.C.: American Psychiatric Press.

Wehrspann, W.H. et al. (1987). Criteria and methodology for assessing credibility of sexual abuse allegation. *Canadian Journal of Psychiatry, 32,* 615-623.

Experience with Alleged Sexual Abuse in Residential Program: II. Problems in the Management of Allegations

Wander de C. Braga, MD

SUMMARY. Problematic areas in the management of allegations of sexual abuse in residential settings are identified and discussed. Areas focused upon are definition, mandated reporting, investigation and allocation of resources. Emphasis is placed on the need to avoid adversarial relationships between residential programs and external monitoring bodies.

The systematic study of sexual abuse in residential and other institutional settings is a very new field. The seminal papers of Thomas (1980), Gil (1982), and Rindfleisch and Rabb (1984) are only a few years old. Initially, the literature stressed the need to avoid denial of this problem. Since then, authors moved to a phase

---

Dr. Braga wishes to express his gratitude to Adele Pickar, MSW, and Susan Parnes for their assistance with the literature search. He may be written at Parsons Child and Family Center, 60 Academy Road, Albany, NY 12208.

[Haworth co-indexing entry note]: "Experience with Alleged Sexual Abuse in Residential Program: II. Problems in the Management of Allegations." Braga, Wander de C. Co-published simultaneously in *Residential Treatment for Children & Youth*, (The Haworth Press, Inc.) Vol. 11, No. 1, 1993, pp. 99-116; and: *Sexual Abuse and Residential Treatment* (ed: Wander de C. Braga, and Raymond Schimmer) The Haworth Press, Inc., 1993, pp. 99-116. Multiple copies of this article/chapter may be purchased from The Haworth Document Delivery Center. Call 1-800-3-HAWORTH (1-800-342-9678) between 9:00 - 5:00 (EST) and ask for DOCUMENT DELIVERY CENTER.

of concern with the motivational and mechanical details of reporting and investigating. Most recently the accent seems to be on the broad systemic factors impinging on the phenomenon of sexual abuse in these settings (Powers, Mooney, & Nunno, 1990; Krantz & Frank, 1990). The latter have stressed the need to change the focus from the abuser to the work organization within which the abuse occurs. They also emphasize the fundamental importance of preserving the residential line worker's sense of dignity, competence, and value, if proper therapeutic work is to occur. Of course, this emphasis must be extended to residential programs as a whole, for they can become devalued, ineffectual and demoralized if alleged sexual abuse in their midst is improperly managed by either internal or external agents.

INCIDENCE AND PREVALENCE

Bloom, Denton and Caflish (1991), from the Illinois Department of Children and Family Services, reported that in the four years from 1986 to 1989 there were 211 allegations of sexual abuse of children in residential programs throughout that state; all cases featured an adult caretaker involvement with a resident. Of these, 57 (27%) were "indicated," which means substantiated after investigation. Unfortunately, the total number of children in placement in such programs was not made available. Therefore, an annual rate of sexual abuse per hundred children cannot be calculated.

The New York Commission on Quality of Care for the Mentally Disabled (February 1992) stated that in residential treatment facilities throughout that state (RTF's), there were 111 reported cases of all types of abuse (not only sexual) in the three years between 1986 and 1989. Of these, 20 incidents referenced an allegation of adult-to-child sexual abuse, while 16 cases involved staff neglect contributing to child-to-child sexual behavior (some individual reports featured multiple and simultaneous allegations). The annual reporting rate for all types of abuse, an average for the three years studied, was 8.68 per hundred children served. The annual averaged reporting rate for adult to child sexual abuse was 1.71 while the reporting rate for staff neglect contributing to child-to-child sexual behavior was 1.16 (per hundred children served per year). The Commission's investigation of the 20 cases involving adults and children resulted in eight cases being "indicated," while of the 16 involving staff neglect, only one was indicated. Thus, the yearly average rate for indicated adult-to-child sexual abuse was 0.73 and the rate for neglect resulting in sexual contact was 0.07 per hundred children. It is important to remark that the author has been cautioned that indications and unfoundings in such cases are highly technical decisions under the law, meaning that the figures above may not necessarily correlate with the reality of what truly happened in the alleged cases.

Groze (1990) studied patterns of institutional abuse in a large southwestern state. He reported that in mental health, child welfare, and correctional facilities during 1985-1987, 40 allegations of sexual abuse occurred, constituting 6.6% of the total abuse allegations. Sexual abuse was defined as any sexual activity prohibited by state law, including sexual exploitation (defined as the use of a child by a person responsible for his health or welfare in sexual activity for personal gratification). Approximately one out of five (22.5%) of the sexual abuse allegations were confirmed, a figure he considered high when compared with the rate of confirmation for other types of abuse. The average age for the victims was 15 years, approximately two-thirds of which were females. Again, the denominator for these figures was not made available, therefore an annual incidence rate per hundred youth cannot be calculated.

In contrast with figures pertaining to residential programs, Finkelhor (1984) reports prevalence figures from a random survey of 521 Boston parents which found that 6% of the males and 15% of the females in the sample studied had an experience of sexual abuse before the age of sixteen with a person at least five years older than themselves. Hartman and Burgess (1991) extrapolated from these figures and stated that a conservative estimate of the national incidence of sexual abuse of children and adolescents is 0.35% per year, which represents 210,000 new cases yearly in the United States!

Prevalence figures were provided by Dubowitz (1986), who estimated that in the population at large as many as 62% of all women had been sexually abused, while some 31% of the men had similar experience in their developmental years.

Valid comparisons between and among the above studies are not possible due to definitional, legal, reporting and methodological problems. More rigorous studies featuring statistics based on operational definitions are needed, in order to compare the rate of sexual abuse in institutions with that in the community at large. However, keeping in mind the currently available figures for institutions (indicated above), a question is raised as to the appropriate match between frequency of this type of incident and the amount of time and energy required for its proper investigation and management. There is no question, however, that preventing such incidents from occurring in the first place is the desired goal.

PROBLEMS IN DEFINITION

Researching the prevalence of sexual abuse in the population at large, Wyat and Peters (1986) pointed out the multiple problems encountered in defining sexual abuse: lack of agreement as to the upper age limit for inclusion, different criteria to define a given experience as abusive, inclusion or exclusion of experiences involving peers, disagreement as to age differential to define peer, etc. Similar concerns were discussed by Giovannoni (1991).

From the perspective of the practitioner of residential treatment, serious difficulties arise when defining as abusive all sexual experiences involving peers. There is no disagreement when an adult staff is clearly involved in a sexual manner with one of his or her charges. Among peers, however, problems occur due to the difficulty in discriminating between normal sexual experimentation or play, sexualized behavior as defined by Gil (1991) and others, and abusive behavior. Gil (1991), borrowing from Groth (1977), defines eight basic issues for distinguishing between the normal, the inappropriate and the clearly abusive and/or assaultive. These are: the age of persons involved; the social relationships; the type of sexual activity; how the sexual contact takes place; how persistent it is; evidence of progression in regard to the nature of frequency of the sexual activity; the nature of fantasies that accompany or precede the sexual behavior; and distinguishing characteristics of persons targeted for sexual activities. These criteria should make it possible

for clinicians to categorize sexual incidents along a spectrum ranging from the normal to the blatantly pathological and/or criminal:
(1) sexual play (small children); (b) sexual contact (older children);
(c) abusive sexual contact; and (d) rape and other forms of sexual
violence. Essential in making these distinctions is the degree of
intimidation, force, coercion or deception involved.

In practice, residential programs attempt to follow the applicable
statues in identifying and reporting alleged abuse. However, these
do not necessarily take into consideration the above-mentioned
clinical criteria. The result is either an inappropriately low threshold
(whereby everything sexual is reported as potentially abusive), or
else there is great confusion when trying to apply the statutes to
unique but frequently ambiguous situations. Johnson (1988) has
taught us that even very small children may molest other children;
Groth (1977) alerted us about the adolescent offender long ago.
There is no question that potential perpetrators do exist among
children and adolescents in our programs. However, it is the presence of intimidation, coercion (implicit when age differential is
significant) and deception that helps separate out the abusive from
the non-abusive cases. It is the viewpoint of this author that line
staff is in the best position to discriminate between abusive and
non-abusive incidents. This is due to their intimate knowledge of
the children involved as well as the complex contextual variables
surrounding an incident. It should follow that a preliminary internal
investigation is of the essence. Examples are plentiful that illustrate
the toxic fall-out that occurs due to definitional difficulties. For
instance, two latency boys run away from the program and go to the
nearby bushes for a sexual experience ("humping"). Frequently
there is no evidence that this encounter fulfills clinically-defined
sexual abuse criteria. Yet, these boys may be taken to an emergency
room for anal and rectal examinations "to obtain evidence." The
boys themselves are unlikely to fail to perceive such medical procedure as excessively punitive and demeaning; further, it may arouse
their anger, guilt and feelings of being abused by the agency. The
need to "obtain evidence" occurs because of the concern that external investigators would demand same. In the absence of such evidence, the agency may be liable for neglect. There is great need for
synchronization of internal and external criteria for sexual abuse;

both must be guided by clinical considerations and, of course, within the spirit of the law. Naturally, this synchronization demands not only clarity of definitions but, most importantly, mutual trust and respect.

Another example, not unfamiliar to staff in most residential programs, is that of teenagers who see themselves "in love," who evade supervision and who engage in sexual intercourse. The girl may find herself sent for an invasive "rape kit," which gives her a clear message as to what the institution thinks about her activity. The boy, if referred for medical exams, will probably be fortunate enough to contend mostly with non-invasive procedures. The rationale for such medico-legal procedures is to gather "evidence" and to "protect health." One needs to ask, how often is non-violent sex physically damaging? Why inject the clients with antibiotics (a common procedure in emergency rooms), when the agency has their medical records and it is known that they are not carriers of infectious diseases? The gynecological exam (also part of the "rape kit") cannot be justified on grounds of pregnancy prevention, as pregnancy is not detected within hours of intercourse; AIDS also cannot be prevented by such procedure. Perhaps those who wish to see such sexual encounters as abusive may not like teenagers to be sexually active.

It is easy to conceive that teenage heterosexual intercourse may bring deleterious consequences (i.e., teen pregnancy and AIDS). However, it seems that teenage consensual intercourse is called sexual abuse only when it occurs in residential or other institutional settings. By defining it as abusive, resident teens are paradoxically discriminated against, rather than protected. Statistics indicate that at least 17% of 13-year-old girls, and 50% of 17-year-old girls in this country have had at least one experience of sexual intercourse. The parents or guardians of these girls are unlikely to submit them to investigators and "rape kits," if they learn of their sexual activities. Their partners are unlikely to be called perpetrators. The point made is that protective mandates affecting teenage sexual contact in residential and other therapeutic facilities have in fact created a new type of "status offense": by demanding that all sexual activity be investigated as though it were abusive, behavior that is rather prevalent in the population at large becomes quasi-criminal and is handled as such.

It is not the intent of the author to argue for the desirability or normalcy of sexual intercourse in adolescence. Rather, one must insist on reasonableness and fairness when handling this matter in residential settings. It merits adding that this problem is not confined to institutionalized children and adolescents. Holbrook (1989), in an article provocatively titled "Policing Sexuality in a Modern State Hospital" cogently describes similar concerns in an adult population of hospitalized developmentally disabled individuals.

PROBLEMS IN DETECTION AND REPORTING

In an effort to educate the public in general and mental health practitioners in particular, lists of symptoms that are purported to be typical of sexual abuse have been advocated. For instance, the official guidelines of the State of New York Department of Social Services and Department of Health (1991) lists regression, overcompliant behavior, withdrawal, lack of trust, difficulty in concentrating at school, overeating, loss of appetite, sleep disorders, unwillingness to allow physical exams, aggressive or disruptive behavior, delinquency, running away, school truancy, substance abuse and other behaviors as possible symptoms of sexual abuse. Of course, a multiplicity of other causes may underlie the above-mentioned symptoms. The seasoned clinician is distressed when confronted with such unspecific and probably overinclusive lists, especially when the need for careful psychiatric assessment to obtain appropriate differential diagnosis is not emphasized.

Agencies, school and other child-serving institutions have been encouraged to offer training to children on how to avoid sexual victimization. This supposedly would facilitate recognition, detection and eventual disclosure of the problem. Such training (e.g., "good touch," "bad touch") may have merit when applied to selected populations. However, the wholesale instruction of the general child population may be unwise. One would need to be concerned about the unintended effects of telling children, especially small ones, that they better be guarded against those entrusted with their care, protection and nurturance. Are small children capable of that type of discrimination? Would this educative effort foster a suspicious and mistrustful attitude towards those who presumably love them? In short, if applied to the population at large, such instruction may contribute to the alienation of affection between non-abused children and their parents or guardians.

A case has been made that even in the recent past our culture has met child sexual abuse with denial, minimization and unwillingness to acknowledge this problem. However, the dramatic explosion of alarm about this matter everywhere, and some of the proposed interventions to solve the problem, should make us wonder if there is a constituency in our society that wishes to see sexual abuse even when there is no reasonable cause to suspect it.

Concerning the reporting of sexual abuse, most states have enacted statutes mandating notification of authorities under conditions of "reasonable suspicion." It may not be easy to define "reasonable" but problems are likely to occur if in practice this word gets translated into "slightest." The problem of thresholds needed to trigger a report surfaces, and then impacts the agency confronted with an allegation. Serious damage can occur when external monitoring bodies deny the agency the prerogative to perform an internal investigation to determine if indeed reasonable suspicion does exist. In the author's experience this occurred in the wake of the enactment of the New York Child Abuse Prevention Act in 1985. However, two or three years afterwards corrective mechanisms apparently prevailed and monitoring bodies no longer are willing to rush investigators to agencies at the slightest suspicion.

It is very disconcerting that some localities prohibit mandated reporters from notifying the alleged perpetrator(s) that a "Hot Line" call for suspected sexual abuse is about to be made. The rationale for such prohibition is that by alerting potential perpetrators, intimidation and coercion of the victim may occur, thereby inhibiting disclosure. To the uninitiated in legal matters, this procedure appears to embody a reversal of a time-honored principle–the accused is innocent until proven guilty. Furthermore, such procedure betrays a lack of concern for its impact on the therapeutic relationship. This must be a matter of apprehension for therapists and therapeutic settings alike.

The ultimate effectiveness of laws that mandate the reporting of sexual and other forms of abuse needs to be carefully studied; it is beyond the scope of this paper to consider the various ramifications of this issue. However, it is noteworthy that the author was unable to locate a single article studying the impact of false accusations of sexual abuse in institutions when, to our best knowledge, four out of five reports fall in this category. From the perspective of non-institutional studies, the prominent child psychiatrist Gardner (1991 and 1992, addendum) has advocated, among other things, that the federal immunity clause (for reporters) be dropped; that the state laws creating mandated reporting be dropped; and that those procedures depriving accused individuals of Constitutional due-process protection be also dropped. Of course, these are far-reaching recommendations that require the best judicial, public policy, and clinical thinking for proper consideration as to ramifications and implications. Perhaps this is a good time to reconsider the path we have traversed in recent years.

Studying residential settings in particular, Rindfleisch and Bean (1988) have pointed out that staff's willingness to report varies with the characteristics of the event, the characteristics of the resident, staff attitudes, etc. Curiously, organizational support for reporting had only minimal influence on the actual willingness to report, but staff commitment to the resident's well being was positively correlated, regardless of threats to one's job or to agency's funding. On the basis of such findings one would think that the best antidote against neglectful non-reporting is the fostering of values such as caring and commitment on the part of staff, which are hallmarks of a good therapeutic setting.

PROBLEMS IN INVESTIGATION

In the management of an allegation of sexual abuse, the investigatory phase is the most sensitive and crucial. The published literature stresses the need for external, independent and specialized bodies to perform this task; it also stresses that such investigations should be systematic as opposed to "ad hoc" (Rindfleisch & Bean, 1988; Nunno & Motz, 1988; Durkin, 1982). The assumption is that faced with residential maltreatment, institutions are likely to respond with denial, cover-up action, defensive behavior, preoccupation with public relations and fear of punitive measures, all of which relate to concerns about damaged reputations, loss of jobs and funding restrictions. One study indicated that the reporting rate of "complainable situations" in institutions was likely to be double than the rate found in families in the community (Rindfleisch & Rabb, 1984). The New York Commission on Quality of Care (1992) gives a yearly reporting rate of all types of abuse as 2.78 per hundred non-institutionalized children in the state, while the comparable rate in RTF's is 8.68. Still in New York, the Department of Social Services (1986) developed a draft manual for conducting child abuse investigations in residential settings. It stressed that the external investigator must have procedural authority to cause medical examination of the child, removal or transfer of same from the facility, transfer or suspension of the alleged perpetrator, immediate change or cessation of particular practices or procedures of the facility, as well as the prerogative to contact law enforcement directly.

Indeed, given the relatively closed-system feature of institutions, the author believes that there is a need for outside investigators to assist in the clarification of facts surrounding an episode of alleged abuse. This is especially so in cases of sexual abuse because frequently these are not accompanied by "hard" physical or corroborative evidence. However, the existence of an external investigatory body is most helpful in that it creates an outside point of reference which helps "neutralize" the complex affective and other job-related interconnections that exist within the human environment of the institution. Personal allegiances, loyalties and also rivalries then take a back seat vis-à-vis an important task: the admittedly unpleasant business of getting an investigation done.

On the other hand, the boundaries of the institution must be respected and protected. A degree of trust between external investigator and the agency must exist. There must be a basic understanding that both are acting to advance the best interests of the youth involved; furthermore, respect, civility and courtesy must characterize transactions between both. Conversely, if outside investigators are possessed of a messianic zeal and a conviction that only they can uncover the facts; if they literally invade residential treatment centers without due regard for staff's views on the alleged event; and if they proceed as though dealing with common criminals, then the reaction of institutions is predictable: they will feel brutalized and demoralized, which will discourage reporting.

The timing of such external investigation is crucial. To repeat, there must be first an opportunity for a preliminary internal investigation to occur–not to cover up and destroy potentially incriminating evidence, but to decide if evidence does exist to support an abuse claim, and to act speedily to protect the potential victim. This viewpoint appears justified not only by the rules of fair play but also by other important variables discussed earlier (i.e., the number of "unfounded" allegations of sexual abuse in residential programs far surpasses the number "indicated"; preliminary statistics suggest that the rate of substantiated cases is not as high as originally suspected and, most importantly, definitional problems do remain, all of which bring a degree of fluidity to the entire process). In short, a cooperative rather than an adversarial process is needed.

It is important to keep in mind that a higher risk of sexual abuse does exist in congregate care of the emotionally disturbed simply because a significant number of former victims and perpetrators are gathered together. Further contributing to increased risk is the estimate that about 70% of the population of residential programs nationally is represented by adolescents (Aldgate, 1987) who are often served by direct line staff (child care workers and teachers) no more than a few years older than themselves. These factors do increase risk. Menzies (1979) has shown that in an agency treating adolescents, the program's unrealistic goals, unsupported by appropriate funding, led to the establishment of what she called an "anti-risk" culture. With the increasing number of sexually abused youth requiring residential treatment, we can ill afford restrictive admission policies so shaped by excessive concern with risk.

A suggested model for investigation of sexual and other types of abuse follows (see Figure 1).

This model is based on a cooperative relationship between internal and external agents, as opposed to an adversarial one. The complexity of this process and its time consuming nature becomes

FIGURE 1

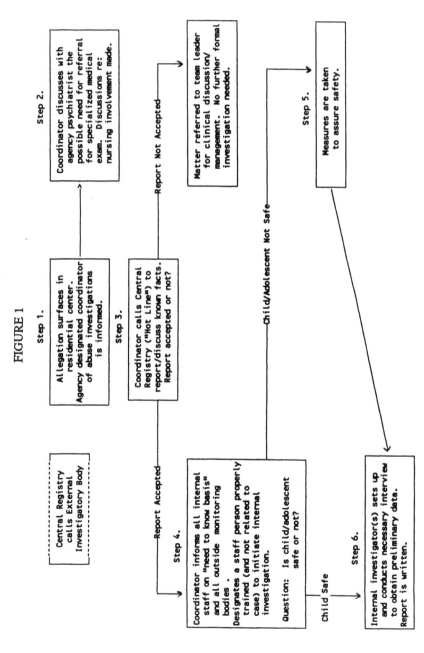

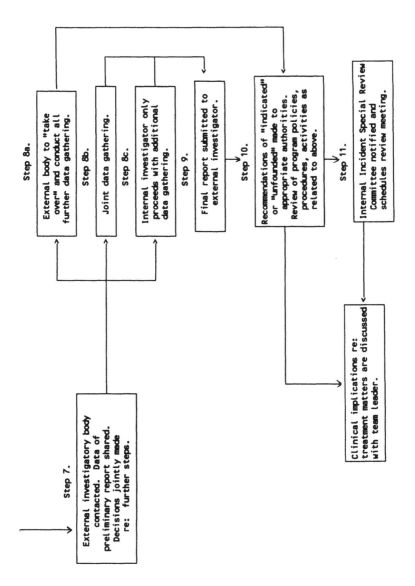

Step 7.

External investigatory body contacted. Data of preliminary report shared. Decisions jointly made re: further steps.

Step 8a.

External body to "take over" and conduct all further data gathering.

Step 8b.

Joint data gathering.

Step 8c.

Internal investigator only proceeds with additional data gathering.

Step 9.

Final report submitted to external investigator.

Step 10.

Recommendations of "indicated" or "unfounded" made to appropriate authorities. Review of program policies, procedures, activities as related to above.

Step 11.

Internal Incident Special Review Committee notified and schedules review meeting.

Clinical implications re: treatment matters are discussed with team leader.

clear even after a brief glance at the schematic figure provided. To facilitate comprehension a few comments are in order.

In step 2, the agency must have a clear protocol as to when to refer children and adolescents for a legally-binding physical examination (the so-called "rape kit"). Again, such exams should not be automatically requested because they are invasive and potentially traumatic. The saying "above all do no harm" is relevant here; medico-legal data of this type should be obtained only for those cases that are clearly indicative of abusive activity or else, when there are well justified concerns about health. In our experience, the bulk of child-to-child sexual activities do not fit these criteria.

In step 4, mention is made of a "need to know" policy. This is a policy that restricts the number of staff informed about the report. Different agencies will articulate it differently. It is the author's experience that in cases of adult-to-child allegations, it is best to notify only the immediate supervisor, team leader and program director, as well as whoever is going to directly be involved in the investigation. Child-to-child cases are more difficult to be contained because the children themselves are likely to spread the "news" all over the program.

In step 5, the decision-making process leading to greater child safety may involve removing or suspending staff from work. This can become rather problematic when local policies demand that the agency refrain from notifying the alleged perpetrator that charges may be filed against him or her.

To properly proceed with step 6, it is important that internal investigators be well trained in obtaining data to support conclusions as to abuse. It is beyond the scope of this paper to describe this type of data-gathering but it merits mentioning that it differs significantly from usual clinical approaches; see Hoorwitz (1992).

The most important feature of this model is step 7. This is an interagency meeting involving outside and inside investigators as well as other relevant personnel. It is at this juncture that a true collaborative stance is operationalized. Based on mutual agreement, the process of obtaining further data is decided upon, while maintaining the welfare of the child as a primary concern.

In step 10, mention is made that external investigators are likely to make recommendations as to policies, procedures, program design and philosophy of treatment. Such recommendations may be legitimate if clearly related to the systemic issues impacting on the emergence of abuse. However, boundaries may be overextended, as monitoring bodies may have their own ideologies, political agendas and philosophies as to what constitutes a desirable service delivery system. Their mandate, however, is to investigate abuse, not redesign treatment programs to conform with preconceived ideologies. Residential settings must resist overarching recommendations that transcend abuse prevention.

FINAL REMARKS

The problem of abuse (sexual and otherwise) in residential settings may be similar to that of refractory infections in the general hospital–the antibiotics used to fight various diseases have "selected" for resistant strains of organisms that have managed to defy even sophisticated and modern medical technology. There is no question that as a form of treatment, the residential modality has its drawbacks as well as its advantages. Pragmatically, one needs to consider the costs versus benefits in assessing its ultimate value. By bringing together children and adolescents who are severely impulsive, who in significant numbers have been sexually abused in their past, and who have very poor frustration-tolerance, one creates a fertile ground that "selects" for all kinds of untoward events. Problems in staffing, in providing adequate coverage, in training and hiring of high quality employees, and in providing optimal organizational support, all contribute to the likelihood that sexual or otherwise, abuse may occur. This is made more complicated by the infiltration of programs by individuals prone to abuse children. Yet, these are the challenges; they are germane to the essential characteristics of congregate care and should be faced with a reasoned attitude and not with a moralistic fervor that invites finger-pointing.

Residential treatment is typically long-term and very expensive. However, ours is a time of diminishing resources, characterized by a preoccupation with cost-cutting and the attainment of "results," that is, objective and measurable outcomes considered desirable by purchasers of services. There is no question that the search for "quick fixes" will accelerate in the near future. Furthermore, key concepts of many leaders in the child welfare field are those of "permanency" and "community treatment." Translated into practice, these concepts foster a view of residential treatment as a problem in itself, rather than a solution for certain problems. In addition, if an assumption is made that abuse (especially sexual abuse) not only exists, but is endemic to such settings, we will witness a resurgence of earlier arguments (Miller, 1981) to close down these institutions. Of course, as pointed out by Thomas (1990), children's institutions have endured for nearly two centuries and when confronted with problems, the public is likely to condemn offending programs (or else to demand that purposes and functions be reformed) rather than advocate for their elimination. Thomas (Ibid.) argues further that institutional abuse must be recognized and realistically approached in its critical characteristics so that something effective can be done to prevent its occurrence. He condemns the shift that has occurred in this country regarding services to children: the basic mission of helping children with growth and development has largely been replaced by services devoted to child protection. To quote him:

> . . . the child-protection oriented message and the set of expectations conveyed to the private child welfare sector, which provides the bulk of institutional services for children, have an adversarial flavor to them. From the perspective of child protection, placements are monitored, first and foremost, to assure that they are protective and not abusive. Mutual suspicion erodes trust thereby undermining the concept of partnership, and the avoidance of any risk that might lead to charges of abuse replaces risk taking among all parties which then erodes the development service mission. (p. 8)

Large is the number of children and adolescents who have been sexually abused and who come to residential programs to be treated, partially because of this insult. It is a monumental challenge for us to figure out effective ways to help this population. Thus, we will need to accept for admission children and adolescents who increase the risk of allegations; only accumulated experience will decide which clients will demand specialized treatment settings. We must get past the adversarialism and recognize that what is needed is broad support for adequately funded quality programs that recognize, manage and deal with sexual and other forms of abuse in a straightforward manner. The ideal of youthful sexual innocence which presumes that children and adolescents need legal protection from all sexual contact must be tempered by the more realistic view that children and adolescents will experiment with sex, and that not all contacts are abusive. We need better methodologies to prevent entry into our programs of adults who are sexually exploitative towards children. What we do not need is an aggressive brand of adversarial and prosecutorial activity which is in turn perceived by service providers as persecutorial, and which undermines morale, trust and effectiveness.

REFERENCES

Aldgate, J. (1987). Residential care: A re-evaluation of a threatened resource. Child and Youth Quarterly, 16 (1), 48-49.

Bloom, R.; Denton, I.R.; & Caflish, C. (1991). Institutional sexual abuse: A crisis in trust. In *Contributions to Residential Treatment*, AACRC, 48-49.

Dubowitz, H. (1986). Child maltreatment in the United States: Etiology, impact and prevention. Background paper prepared for the United States Congress, Office of Technology Assessment.

Durkin, R. (1982). No one will thank you: First thoughts on reporting institutional abuse. In Hanson, R. (Ed.), *Institutional Abuse of Children*. New York: The Haworth Press, Inc.

Finkelhor, D. (1984). *Child sexual abuse: New theories and research*. New York: Free Press.

Gardner, R.A. (1991). *Sex abuse hysteria: Salem witch trials revisited*. Cresskill, NJ: Creative Therapeutics.

Gardner, R.A. (1992). *True and false accusations of child sex abuse*. Cresskill, NJ: Creative Therapeutics.

Gil, E. (1982). Institutional abuse of children in out-of-home care. Child and Youth Care Review, 4 (1-2), 7-13.

Gil, E. (1991). Defining and responding to sexualized children. In *Contributions to Residential Treatment*, AACRC, 53-59.

Giovannoni, J. (1991). Definitional issues in child maltreatment. In Cicchetti, D. & Carlson, V. (Eds.), *Child maltreatment*. Cambridge University Press, 3-37.

Groth, A.N. (1977). The adolescent sex offender and his prey. International Journal of Offender Therapy and Comparative Criminology, 21, 249-254.

Groze, V. (1990). An exploratory investigation into institutional mistreatment. Child and Youth Services Review, 12, 229-241.

Hartman, C.R. & Burgess, A.W. (1991). Sexual abuse of children: Causes and consequences. In Cicchetti, D. & Carlson, V. (Eds.), *Child maltreatment.* Cambridge University Press, 95-127.

Holbrook, T. (1989). Policing sexuality in a modern state hospital. Hospital and Community Psychiatry, *4* (1), 75-79.

Hoorwitz, N.A. (1992). *The clinical detective* New York: W.W. Norton.

Johnson, T.C. (1988). Child perpetrators–children who molest other children: Preliminary findings. Child Abuse and Neglect, 12, 219-229.

Miller, J.G. (1981). Thoughts on institutional abuse. Legal Response: Child Advocacy and Protection, 2, 13.

New York Commission on Quality of Care for the Mentally Disabled (1992). Child abuse and neglect in New York State, Office of Mental Health and Office of Mental Retardation and Developmental Disabilities Residential Programs.

New York State Department of Social Services (1986). Draft manual for conducting child abuse investigations in residential child care.

Nunno, M. & Motz, J. (1988). The development of an effective response to the abuse of children in out-of-home care. Child Abuse and Neglect, 12, 521-528.

Powers, J.L.; Mooney, A. & Nunno, M. (1990). Institutional abuse: A review of the literature. Journal of Child and Youth Care, 4 (6), 81-95.

Rindfleisch, N. & Bean, J. (1988). Willingness to report abuse and neglect in residential facilities. Child Abuse and Neglect, 12, 509-520.

Rindfleisch, N. & Rabb, J. (1984). How much of a problem is resident maltreatment in child welfare institutions? Child Abuse and Neglect, 8, 33-40.

State of New York Department of Social Services and Department of Health (1991). Suspected child abuse and maltreatment: Identification and management in hospitals and clinics (official guidelines).

Thomas, G. (1980). Dimensions of the problem of child abuse and neglect in residential placement that distinguish it from child abuse and neglect in the family context. Testimony before U.S. House of Representatives, December 4.

Thomas, G. (1990). Institutional child abuse: The making and prevention of an un-problem. Journal of Child and Youth Care, 4 (6), 1-22.

Wyat, G.E. & Peters, S.D. (1986). Issues in the definition of child abuse in prevalence research. Child Abuse and Neglect, 10, 231-240.

Index

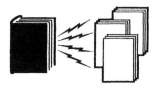

Haworth
DOCUMENT DELIVERY
SERVICE
and Local Photocopying Royalty Payment Form

This new service provides (a) a single-article order form for any article from a Haworth journal and (b) a convenient royalty payment form for local photocopying (not applicable to photocopies intended for resale).

- *Time Saving:* No running around from library to library to find a specific article.
- *Cost Effective:* All costs are kept down to a minimum.
- *Fast Delivery:* Choose from several options, including same-day FAX.
- *No Copyright Hassles:* You will be supplied by the original publisher.
- *Easy Payment:* Choose from several easy payment methods.

Open Accounts Welcome for...
- Library Interlibrary Loan Departments
- Library Network/Consortia Wishing to Provide Single-Article Services
- Indexing/Abstracting Services with Single Article Provision Services
- Document Provision Brokers and Freelance Information Service Providers

MAIL or *FAX* THIS ENTIRE ORDER FORM TO:

Attn: **Marianne Arnold**
Haworth Document Delivery Service
The Haworth Press, Inc.
10 Alice Street
Binghamton, NY 13904-1580

or **FAX:** (607) 722-1424
or **CALL:** 1-800-3-HAWORTH
(1-800-342-9678; 9am-5pm EST)

PLEASE SEND ME PHOTOCOPIES OF THE FOLLOWING SINGLE ARTICLES:
1) Journal Title: _____
   Vol/Issue/Year: _____ Starting & Ending Pages: _____
   Article Title: _____
   _____

2) Journal Title: _____
   Vol/Issue/Year: _____ Starting & Ending Pages: _____
   Article Title: _____
   _____

3) Journal Title: _____
   Vol/Issue/Year: _____ Starting & Ending Pages: _____
   Article Title: _____
   _____

4) Journal Title: _____
   Vol/Issue/Year: _____ Starting & Ending Pages: _____
   Article Title: _____
   _____

(See other side for Costs and Payment Information)

COSTS: Please figure your cost to order quality copies of an article.

1. Set-up charge per article: $8.00
   ($8.00 × number of separate articles) _____

2. Photocopying charge for each article:
   1-10 pages: $1.00 _____
   11-19 pages: $3.00 _____
   20-29 pages: $5.00 _____
   30+ pages: $2.00/10 pages _____

3. Flexicover (optional): $2.00/article _____

4. Postage & Handling: US: $1.00 for the first article/
   $.50 each additional article _____
   Federal Express: $25.00 _____
   Outside US: $2.00 for first article/
   $.50 each additional article _____

5. Same-day FAX service: $.35 per page _____

6. Local Photocopying Royalty Payment: should you wish to copy the article yourself. Not intended for photocopies made for resale. $1.50 per article per copy (i.e. 10 articles x $1.50 each = $15.00) _____

GRAND TOTAL: _____

METHOD OF PAYMENT: (please check one)

❏ Check enclosed   ❏ Please ship and bill. PO # _____
(sorry we can ship and bill to bookstores only! All others must pre-pay)

❏ Charge to my credit card: ❏ Visa;   ❏ MasterCard;   ❏ American Express;

Account Number:_____ Expiration date:_____

Signature: *X*_____ Name: _____

Institution: _____ Address: _____

City: _____ State:_____ Zip:_____

Phone Number: _____ FAX Number: _____

MAIL or *FAX* THIS ENTIRE ORDER FORM TO:

Attn: **Marianne Arnold**
Haworth Document Delivery Service
The Haworth Press, Inc.
10 Alice Street
Binghamton, NY 13904-1580

or **FAX:** (607) 722-1424
or **CALL:** 1-800-3-HAWORTH
(1-800-342-9678; 9am-5pm EST)